MATRIMONIAL CONVEYANCING:

A Draftsman's Handbook

Fifth Edition

William M Hartley
MA (Cantab), Solicitor

© Longman Group UK Ltd 1993

ISBN 0-85121-939-X

Published by
Longman Group UK Ltd
21–27 Lamb's Conduit Street
London WC1N 3NJ

Associated offices
Australia, Hong Kong, Malaysia, Singapore and USA

First published 1981
Fifth Edition 1993

A CIP catalogue record for this book is available
from the British Library.

Printed in Great Britain by
Bell and Bain Ltd, Glasgow.

MATRIMONIAL CONVEYANCING

Contents

Precedents

Foreword

When I arrived in the profession as an Articled Clerk in 1966 it was still just about possible to imagine a career in the solicitors profession as a jack of all trades. After all one had just been taught property law, company law, family law and a host of other subjects and really no-one had indicated that passing most of these exams had been an academic exercise. Within two or three years, however, it became apparent that the move towards specialisation in the profession was absolutely unstoppable. One result has been that most family lawyers find it very difficult to draft conveyancing documents.

I myself had the good fortune to cling on to three subjects for a time namely, family law, administration of estates and conveyancing.

Nevertheless in spite of my familiarity with the subject I recall having the most enormous difficulty in preparing the documents that are so excellently set out in this book. It was not until 1982 that a colleague mentioned the existence of Hartley's Matrimonial Conveyancing and the ease with which my firm has coped with these matters ever since has been remarkable.

The important point is that family lawyers have every reason to feel confident that with this book at their elbow; they need not incur the delay and expense of troubling their conveyancing colleagues to ask them to prepare documents of this nature. This can now be regarded as a straightforward task as a result of Mr. Hartley's efforts.

The book is wholly practical. It has obviously been prepared by an author of great experience who knows and understands what the practitioner wants. That is not an observation that I would make in relation to many other precedents commonly to be found in solicitor's offices.

J. R. Cornwell LLB
London 1993

Preface

The first edition of this book was prompted by the increasing number of conveyances that the author had to draft following or during the course of matrimonial proceedings between a husband and wife. Many of the well-established text-books contained precedents relating to a conveyance of a share of joint property but fell short of providing precedents for the situations commonly occurring in relation to the matrimonial home.

The earlier editions aimed to fill that gap by providing precedents that could easily be adapted to meet particular circumstances together with practical comment.

This edition expands the precedents and comment having regard to recent developments both in the courts and in practice. The precedents are presented in a more modern format.

It is thought that the introduction of the Child Support Act 1991 will limit the willingness of the supporting husband to agree to a clean break and transfer of the matrimonial home to the wife, but it remains to be seen what arrangements in practice will evolve.

My thanks are due to those who have written to me or to the publishers with their comments and suggestions. It was gratifying to learn that the book continues to meet a need in many solicitors' offices.

The law is stated as at 1 April 1993.

April 1993
Manchester   *William M Hartley*

Table of Cases

Table of Statutes

Table of Statutory Instruments

Chapter 1

General Principles

The petition for divorce is nowadays rarely contested by the respondent. By contrast, the future of the matrimonial home is often a keenly fought issue for it is usually the major capital asset possessed either jointly by the parties to the marriage or by one of them.

The importance of the matrimonial home has been recognised increasingly by the legislature. Since the first edition of this book both the Matrimonial Homes (Co-ownership) Bill introduced in the House of Lords in 1980 (which would have made provision for statutory co-ownership of the matrimonial home) and the Land Registration of Law of Property Bill (affecting the practice that has grown up following the case of *Williams & Glyn's Bank Ltd v Boland*) [1981] AC 487) have failed. However since that date parliament has passed the Matrimonial Homes and Property Act 1981, the Matrimonial Homes Act 1983 and the Matrimonial and Family Proceedings Act 1984. Faced with legislation on this scale, the bias towards the 'clean break' encouraged by the courts and the Matrimonial and Family Proceedings Act 1984 and the trend of increased home ownership, it is apparent that orders and arrangements concerning the matrimonial home can only increase.

1 The scope of this book

The first edition of this book assumed a conveyance or transfer of the matrimonial home following a court order or agreement in matrimonial proceedings. Whilst this edition still primarily addresses that situation it also deals with the conveyance of the matrimonial home in other situations, for instance the insolvency of the husband (see Chapter 10) and, following his death, a claim by the wife against his estate.

1

In its treatment of matrimonial conveyancing, this book is not concerned with the merits of the spouses' respective claims nor with the proceedings in connection with those claims. It deals with the necessary conveyancing following the making of a court order or agreement between the parties relating to the matrimonial home and with the disentangling of life policies should that be necessary. The book is not confined to the needs of the conveyancing practitioner, however; it is thought that the divorce practitioner should also have knowledge of the different types of conveyance which may be ordered by the court or agreed between the parties and the points which should be taken into account at that time, the protective measures that might be taken before the conveyance is concluded and the documentation that may be required in dealing with life policies.

In the precedents which follow the husband is treated as the transferor or conveying party, since this is the more common case, although no discrimination is intended!

This chapter touches on various points of which the practitioner should be aware, which may usefully serve as a reminder of items to be considered outside the drafting of the conveyance or transfer itself.

2 The advantage of a court order

Although agreement may be reached between the parties as to the future of the matrimonial home, it is strongly advised that such agreement be embodied in a 'consent order' of the court; if the court does not have the power directly to make an order under the Matrimonial Causes Act 1973 (for instance in relation to repairs to property held subject to certain conditions and in relation to payment of premiums of life assurance policies) the same effect can be achieved by formulating the obligations of each party as undertakings given to the court (see *Livesey v Jenkins* [1985] 1 All ER 106 and Salter, *Matrimonial Consent Orders and Agreements*, 2nd edn, Longman 1991). Indeed, because of the court's limited power, the policy of ultimate caution must be for the terms of any conveyancing documentation to be agreed between the respective solicitors before the consent order is applied for.

Such an order has inheritance tax advantages (if dissolution of the marriage has taken place), a saving in the HM Land Registry fees is available (see Chapter 3 and generally) and, as any financial provision can be expressed in the order to be in full and final settlement of the wife's claims (see Chapter 11), it is less likely to be upset than an agreement between the parties not carried into a 'consent order' (see for instance *Dinch v Dinch* [1987] 1 WLR 252 where the court refused to make a further order on the grounds that the consent order had conclusively determined the rights of the parties in the matrimonial home). A court order avoids the repayment of the discount on the transfer of a former council house (see further this chapter) and it is only by court order (with the agreement of the parties) that future claims against the estate of one party to the former marriage can be barred out (see Chapter 11).

3 Property subject to a mortgage

In many cases a mortgage will affect the property, and depending upon the terms of the court order or agreement the requirements of the mortgagee should be observed.

An application for a property adjustment order is required to identify the land, specify whether the property concerned is registered or unregistered (and, if the former, its title number), and give particulars (as far as known to the applicant) of the mortgage (for example the mortgage account number and the full names of the mortgagor(s)) (Family Proceedings Rules 1991 (SI No 1247) r 2.59(2)). A copy of the prescribed Form M11 or M13 (as the case may be) is required to be sent to the mortgagee (r 2.59(4)).

It is, of course, not legally necessary for a mortgagee to be joined in a conveyance of the equity in the property; however, without the title documents a conveyance of an unregistered title subject to a mortgage from husband to wife cannot be safely undertaken. No such problems prevent such a conveyance where registered title is involved since office copy entries of the title can be obtained and the transfer once executed by the husband and wife can be lodged at HM Land Registry. In the latter case, the registrar is bound to register the transfer as he holds the land certificate (in contrast to the charge certificate, which is held by the mortgagee) unless there is a restriction on the proprietorship register requiring the consent of the mortgagee to such transfer.

More commonly, however, one party to the original mortgage is to be released or another party added, and in these cases it is necessary for the mortgagee concerned to be a party to the document (unless separate deeds of release and covenant are executed). The terms of the mortgage may in any event require that the mortgagee be joined as a party to any document affecting the property subject to the charge in its favour, and in registered conveyancing there may be a restriction to this effect on the proprietorship register. In practice, therefore, where a mortgage affects the property the mortgagee will be a party to the conveyance or transfer.

Some mortgagees have standard clauses that they require to be inserted in the conveyance or transfer of the property charged in their favour and some mortgagees require to approve the draft document, whilst others (for instance, the Halifax Building Society) delegate the task of drafting to the mortgagee's solicitor with a few suggested (but by no means mandatory) clauses. It is therefore advisable to check the particular mortgagee's requirements before finalising any documentation.

Regard must be had to the decision in *Williams & Glyn's Bank Ltd v Boland* [1981] AC 487. The case highlighted the difficulty facing a mortgagee when a person other than its borrower lives at the mortgaged premises, for such person, as confirmed by this case, may have rights or interests in that property (although the principles of the case are not being so strictly applied as was first thought—see *Bristol & West Building Society v Henning* [1985] 2 All ER 606 and *Midland Bank Ltd v Dobson* (1985) NLJ 26 July, 251). Most mortgagees have required specific consent from such persons to the taking of a charge by the mortgagee over the property or where they consent to a transfer of the property subject to the mortgage, coupled with confirmation from such persons that their rights are postponed to those of the mortgagee under its mortgage. Many mortgagees have issued standard forms of consent for completion in such circumstances (and see Precedent 11).

If the mortgage is additionally secured by the assignment of a life policy, then the future of that policy must be sorted out. If the matrimonial home is to be transferred to the sole name of the wife the mortgagee may be content to re-assign a life policy on the life of the husband to him, the mortgage on the property reverting to a repayment mortgage. Alternatively the benefit of the policy may pass to the wife, subject to charge. This is dealt with more fully in Chapter 9.

4 Tax

It is a fact of modern legal practice that the tax aspects of every transaction should be considered. This book does not claim to treat this topic exhaustively but focuses attention on the major heads of charge as a reminder of the possible tax consequences of transactions covered in this book (see Chapter 2).

Each case will of course depend on its facts; regard should be had to any possible tax consequences before the court order or agreement between the parties is finalised.

5 Council Tax

The 4th edition of this book commented briefly on the Community Charge introduced by the Local Government Finance Act 1988. The charge or poll tax as it was commonly called was abolished as from 31 March 1993. (Local Government Finance Act 1992, Sched 14).

With effect from 1 April 1993 a dwelling will be subject to the Council Tax and the full amount is payable where there are two or more adult residents. The liable person will normally be the resident who owns the property (s 75); joint owners are jointly liable as is the resident spouse of a liable person (s 77).

If there is only one adult resident, a discount of 25 per cent can be claimed (s 79); it is important therefore that if husband and wife cease to live together each of them should notify the local authority that separation has taken place so as to end joint liability and for the remaining resident spouse to claim the discount (if applicable).

6 Insolvency

Practitioners will be aware that transactions at an undervalue can be put aside (Insolvency Act 1986, s 339) if the transferor is adjudged bankrupt within two years of the transaction or if he becomes bankrupt within five years of the transaction and was insolvent at that time or was insolvent by reason of it (s 341).

It is difficult to say whether or not a transfer of a house by the husband to the wife in, for instance, a 'clean break' is 'less in money or money's worth than the value in money or money's worth of the consideration provided' (s 339(3)(c)) so there is always a risk that a conveyance or transfer following the court order or agreement may be attacked by a husband's trustee in bankruptcy and the wife cannot be absolutely safe until the five year period has expired. There is nothing in the Act to confer immunity on a conveyance or transfer carried out to comply with a court order, but the existence of the wife's right to financial relief against her husband may provide sufficient value to prevent the transaction being at an undervalue within the context of the Insolvency Act 1986 (see Berry and Bailey, *Bankruptcy Law and Practice* Butterworths 1987, p 294).

In *Re Abbott* (a bankrupt) [1983] Ch 45 (a case decided before the Insolvency Act 1986) a wife's petition for divorce sought an order transferring the jointly owned matrimonial home to her. Agreement was reached and a consent order subsequently made to the effect that the house should be sold and that the husband should pay the wife a lump sum of £9,000 from his share of the proceeds of sale. On the husband's bankruptcy within two years of the consent order, the Trustee sought to recover £9,000 from the wife, that sum being the amount in excess of the value of her half share in the house. The Court held that she was a purchaser for valuable consideration, the consideration being the withdrawal of a *bona fide* claim to a property adjustment order.

It was thought that amending legislation would be introduced (*Practical Lawyer*, June 1990, p 11) but until it is, in addition to the risk of the conveyance or transfer with respect to the matrimonial home being set aside, the wife may find it difficult to sell the property (although the Law Society takes the view that there is 'very little risk that a Court would exercise its powers to deprive an innocent owner of his title.' See *Law Society's Gazette* 5 February 1992, p 13). One could attempt to limit the 'period of difficulty' to the two years by having a declaration of solvency (if applicable) sworn by the husband at the same time as he makes the conveyance (see Chapter 10, Precedent 81) and hope that that is acceptable to a prospective purchaser from the wife between the expiry of the two years and five year period.

There is the further difficulty that mortgagees, in circumstances where there might have been a conveyance or transfer at less than full consideration (whatever that is in a matrimonial context), are requiring indemnity insurance to protect the mortgagee for an amount equal to the advance (see Halifax Building Society practice notes 1992 paras 22 and 25). Insurers usually require a Statutory Declaration as to the solvency of the transferor husband at the time of the conveyance so the practitioner must consider whether or not it is practical to ask for this at the time of the conveyance (see further Chapter 10).

As far as registered land is concerned, HM Land Registry have confirmed that in their view, a transfer of property made in order to comply with a property adjustment order falls within the scope of s 339. This practice is under review (*Law Society's Gazette*, 25 January 1989). Presently, no entry relating to the section will be entered on the register if the land is already registered because a transferee of registered land made under a disposition without valuable consideration is subject to minor interests (such as rights of creditors) (see Land Registration Act 1925 ss 20(4) and 23(5)). Although the practice appears to vary, an entry may be entered on the proprietorship register, however, in the following form:

> Note: The land having been acquired under a voluntary conveyance dated   made by [*donor*] the registered title is subject to the provisions of section 339 Insolvency Act 1986

if there is a purchase at an undervalue of unregistered land in a compulsory registration area. A prospective purchaser would presumably be hesitant to proceed in such circumstances without adequate insurance protection.

7 Practice of HM Land Registry

Rule 74 of the Land Registration Rules 1925 (SR & O 1925 No 1093) (set out in full in Ruoff and Roper, *Registered Conveyancing*, Looseleaf edn, Sweet and Maxwell, 1991) specifies that the forms set out in the Schedule to those Rules shall be used where appropriate to the particular transaction concerned.

Where no form is prescribed for a transaction, or a prescribed form cannot be conveniently adapted, r 75 provides that the instrument shall be in such form as the registrar shall direct or allow but shall follow the approved forms as nearly as possible. It will be appreciated that this rule gives the registrar a wide discretion. The forms set out in this book follow the prescribed forms as nearly as circumstances permit and it is thought that they will be acceptable to HM Land Registry.

HM Land Registry fees are mentioned throughout the book. It will be readily appreciated that these can be subject to change.

8 Class F Land Charge (or Notice if registered land)

No book relating to matrimonial home conveyancing would be complete without mention of the Class F Land Charge, or its registered land equivalent. Although the registration of the charge precedes the situation covered in this book, and is thus more within the ambit of the practitioner advising in the initial stages of matrimonial proceedings than the conveyancer, a reminder of the requirements and consequences of registration is relevant.

The Matrimonial Homes Act 1983, which has almost entirely replaced the Matrimonial Homes Act 1967 which introduced the Class F Land Charge, gives a spouse who is not entitled to occupy a dwelling house by virtue of a beneficial estate or interest or contract, the right (if in occupation) not to be evicted or excluded therefrom except by order of the court and the right (if not in occupation) with the leave of the court to enter into and occupy the dwelling house.

Such a right is protected by registration of a Class F Land Charge or a Notice at HM Land Registry if the matrimonial home has registered title. Registration at HM Land Registry is required to be made in Form 99 (The Land Registration (Matrimonial Homes) Rules 1990 SI No 1360) (no fee required); an official search of the index map at HM Land Registry (Form 96) will need to be made to see if the land is registered unless the position is known without doubt. (Fee £8.00 – The Land Registration Fees Order 1992 (SI No 2089.)

An alternative procedure which appears to be acceptable to HM Land Registry is to apply for office copies of the registered title (Form 109); this incurs the same fee (£8) as an index map search, and following the Land Registration (Open Register)

Rules 1991 it is not necessary to specify the name of the proprietor; if the land is not registered the application will be rejected, but if it is registered the receipt of office copies gives the opportunity to check the charges register for mortgages. Strictly one should specify if one is requiring the freehold or leasehold title, but in practice to tick both boxes seems to work (unless the position is obvious, such as with a flat).

As far as registered title is concerned, the land certificate need not be produced (Land Registration Act 1925, s 64(5) added by Matrimonial Homes and Property Act 1981, s 4(1)). There is no fee payable for the registration of a notice under the Matrimonial Homes Act 1983 (Land Registration Fees Order 1992 (SI No 2089), Sched 4, exemption 4).

It is important to appreciate that the Matrimonial Homes Act 1983 only applies to a dwelling house which has been the matrimonial home (s 1(10)). Thus if husband and wife live together in one house, a Class F Land Charge or Notice cannot effectively be registered against a house owned solely by the husband and in which he has installed his mistress.

A Class F Land Charge or Notice is binding on a husband's trustee in bankruptcy, subject to the provisions of the Matrimonial Homes Act (Insolvency Act 1986, s 336).

The rights of occupation come to an end on the death of the other spouse or on the termination of the marriage (s 2(4)) unless the court has ordered otherwise. Thus the production of a death certificate, decree absolute or other court order should ensure the cancellation of the land charge (s 5(1)) or notice. (HM Land Registry Form 202.)

In a disputed property case, because the Class F effectively comes to an end on the issue of the decree absolute protective steps mentioned in the next section should be taken.

It should be appreciated that if one party to the marriage has no wish to occupy the matrimonial home that party is not entitled to register a Class F Land Charge against the owner (see *Barnett v Hassett* [1981] 1 WLR 1385 where the husband left the wife's house and did not wish to occupy it).

It should be remembered that any contract for sale which provides for the purchaser to obtain vacant possession on completion now implies a provision that the vendor will procure before completion the cancellation of a registered Class F Land

Charge (Matrimonial Homes Act 1983, s 4(1)). Notwithstanding this provision, it is often of some reassurance to a purchaser from the husband if the wife is joined as a party to the contract or to a separate consent to sale form; this confirms that she knows that vacant possession is to be given and the land charge is to be cancelled and can contain a specific release by the wife of her rights in the property as from the date of sale. Negotiations between the husband and wife will often have been on the basis that the wife's solicitors will hand over an application for cancellation of the land charge (Form K13 or application for the cancellation of the notice if registered land Form 202) on completion in return for one-half of the net proceeds of sale (or whatever other figure is agreed).

Any such application must be signed by the wife (see the negligence case of *Holmes v Kennard* (1984) 128 SJ 854) if her rights of occupation have not otherwise come to an end. Form K13 and HM Land Registry Form 202 makes provision for this.

9 Protection of the wife's position before completion of conveyance to her or lodging of transfer for registration

To avoid the husband making a sale or charging the property (standing in his sole name) in the period between the decree absolute (when the Class F protection ceases—see above) and the completion of the conveyance to the wife or lodging of the transfer at HM Land Registry:

(a) Unregistered Land

A pending action under s 5 of the Land Charges Act 1972 (fee £1.00) should be registered by or on behalf of the wife (in Form K3) provided the divorce petition has contained a request for a transfer of real property under s 24 of the Matrimonial Causes Act 1973; such a registration survives the decree absolute (see *Whittingham v Whittingham* [1978] 2 WLR 936 and *Perez-Adamson v Perez-Rivas* [1987] 2 WLR 500).

The pending action land charge should effectively stop the husband dealing with the property until completion of the conveyance in the wife's favour has taken place and she is in receipt of the title deeds, for any purchaser or mortgagee will be put on notice by the entry at HM Land Charges Registry.

It is too late to register a pending action if a bankruptcy petition has been presented against the husband; in *Re Flint* (1992) *The Times* 16 July it was held that a transfer of the matrimonial home by order of the court in matrimonial proceedings to the wife in the period between the presentation of a bankruptcy petition against the husband and the bankruptcy order was void.

(b) Registered Land

A caution should be lodged at HM Land Registry (Fee £40, Land Registration Fees Order 1992 (SI No 2089), Sched 3, Pt II).

Form 63 requires a statutory declaration (in Form 14) by either the cautioner or her solicitor disclosing the nature of the cautioner's interest.

i) In the case where a court order has not yet been made, the nature of the cautioner's interest may be shown as:

> the former wife of the registered proprietor having made application for a property adjustment order under s 24 Matrimonial Causes Act 1973 by proceedings in the [*Manchester*] County Court between [*husband*] and [*wife*] bearing number of matter

ii) In the case where the court order in favour of the wife has been made, but the transfer has not yet been executed and lodged in HM Land Registry and no earlier caution has been registered this might be:

> the registered proprietor [*husband*] has been ordered to transfer all his estate and interest in the property to [*wife*] by an order made in the [*Manchester*] County Court dated in proceedings between [*husband*] and [*wife*] bearing number of matter

Unless a caution is registered there is risk; before lodging the transfer the wife's solicitor will make a Form 94C search, but such search does not confer priority for the registration of any dealing (Land Registration (Official Searches) Rules 1990 (SI No 1361), r 9). Some practitioners make a Form 94A search which gives priority in favour of a purchaser, taking the view that the wife is the equivalent of a purchaser. HM Land Registry have indicated that this priority might fail in the event of the lodging of a valid charge by the husband's mortgagee, as strictly the wife is not, in their view, a purchaser for valuable consideration.

10 Former council houses

A good number of people have purchased the houses in which they live from the Local Authority or New Town Development Corporations under the provisions of the Housing Act 1985. The disposal of such dwelling house within three years (Housing and Planning Act 1986, s 2(3)) from the date of purchase 'triggers' repayment of the discount on the proportion still outstanding by reference to the number of years since purchase but s 160(1)(c) of the Act, specifically exempts from the repayment provisions disposals in pursuance of an order under s 24 of the Matrimonial Causes Act 1973, where continued occupation is envisaged (see *R v Rushmoor Borough Council ex p Barrett* [1987] 1 All ER 353).

Thus an order of the court that a former council house or New Town Development House be transferred to one party of the marriage will not necessitate at the time of the transfer repayment of the discount or any part of it allowable at the time of purchase.

Liability to repay the discount is secured by the registration of a notice or caution at HM Land Registry (Housing Act 1985, s 156) and any transfer to the wife will of course be subject to such notice or caution. The question of unregistered land does not arise because any such purchase is subject to compulsory registration of title (Housing Act 1985, s 154).

11 Execution of documents

Section 1 of the Law of Property (Miscellaneous Provisions) Act 1989 specifies that if an instrument is to be a deed, this must be clear on the face of it, and that the requirement for individuals to seal is abolished. Sealing after that date does not invalidate the deed; the presence of a seal is merely superfluous to the requirements for execution. Section 130 of the Companies Act 1989 contains corresponding provisions relating to the sealing of deeds by companies registered under the Companies Acts.

The Land Registration (Execution of Deeds) Rules 1990 (SI No 1010) introduced the present Form 19 (transfer of freehold land) in the Schedule to the Land Registration Rules 1925. All other deeds relating to registered land are required to follow the same form of execution as Form 19.

12 Legal Aid Statutory Charge

Under s 16 of the Legal Aid Act 1988, if the Legal Aid Board suffers a deficiency in respect of an assisted person's proceedings (ie they have paid more to the assisted person's legal advisers than they have received by way of costs from the other side and from contributions paid) the statutory charge may attach to money or property 'recovered' or 'preserved' that has been 'in issue' in the course of proceedings.

Periodical payments of maintenance escape the statutory charge as does the first £2,500 of any money or property preserved or recovered (Civil Legal Aid (General) Regulations 1989, reg 94). Hence, if a lump sum is recovered over £2,500 the charge will attach to the balance and the Legal Aid Board can seek immediate repayment of its deficiency from that.

If, however, the court order specifies that the lump sum is to be used for the purpose of purchasing a home for the assisted person or her dependants enforcement of the charge can be postponed (Civil Legal Aid (General) Regulations 1989, reg 96). Similarly if the property recovered or preserved is to be used as a home for the assisted person or her dependants enforcement of the charge can also be postponed. As to the certificate to be contained in the Court Order to obtain such postponement see Practice Direction [1991] 1 WLR 955. In each case the Legal Aid Board will register a land charge on the former matrimonial home or the home bought with the lump sum:

(a) Unregistered land

The Board will register a Class B land charge within the meaning of the Land Charges Act 1972, s 2 (reg 95).

(b) Registered land

The Board will register either a substantive charge or a notice or caution, depending upon the practice of the individual Board. This might be as follows: 'Caution in favour of the Legal Aid Board of   registered on   '. If the charge is registered after 1 December 1988 the charge, if postponed, will carry simple interest presently at the rate of 10.5 per cent per annum (reg 97).

Normally the charge will be repaid when the property is sold but the Board has a discretion to transfer it to a substitute property in certain limited circumstances (see reg 98). Correspondence concerning redemption or transfer should be addressed to Legal Aid Accounts Department, Land Charge Section 12 Roger St, London WC1N 2JL quoting the full name and address of the assisted person, civil legal aid certificate number, title number or land charge department reference number (*Law Society's Gazette* No 17, 6 May 1992).

Chapter 2

The Tax Aspects

The practitioner acting for the husband should consider the tax effect of any transfer of the matrimonial home, or interest therein, to the other party to the marriage, and upon whom the burden of any taxation is to fall.

In all circumstances relating to tax matters it must be appreciated that each set of facts is to be looked at separately. The contents of this chapter cannot describe the tax position on each transfer; they can only draw attention to the possible heads of charge and reliefs available in respect of each of them.

1 Mortgage interest relief

In considering the payment of income maintenance, regard should be had to any mortgage interest which has to be paid if the matrimonial home is retained and to the most tax advantageous method of payment for both husband and wife.

Interest paid under a mortgage is allowable for tax relief if at the time the interest is paid:

(i) the loan was taken out to purchase property in the UK; and

(ii) the person claiming the relief owed an interest in the property and uses it 'wholly or to a substantial extent' as his or her only or main residence (Income and Corporation Taxes Act 1988, ss 354 and 355 as amended by Finance Act 1988, s 44(1)).

Thus, if there is an outright transfer of the matrimonial home to the wife subject to the existing mortgage (see Chapters 3, 4 and 7) or the matrimonial home is held on certain terms and conditions (see Chapter 6) then the occupant wife should be made responsible for the mortgage payments (the husband would not be using

15

the house as his only or main residence and so would not be eligible for interest relief).

The relief is only available up to £30,000 per residence (Income and Corporation Taxes Act 1988, s 367(5); Finance Act 1990, s 71). See further Whitehouse and Stuart-Buttle, *Revenue Law* (10th edn, Butterworth, pp 656, 673).

The Finance Act 1993 introduces limits on the relief effective from 6 April 1994.

2 Capital gains tax

Prima facie if a disposal of the former matrimonial home or an interest therein occurs, there is a charge to capital gains tax. It is important therefore to have a look at the reliefs and exemptions that may be available.

The rate of tax on chargeable gains is that which results from adding the gain to the individual's total income. The gain may be taxed at the basic rate of income tax therefore or at the higher rate. A non-resident is not liable to capital gains tax (see further *Revenue Law*, p 317).

(a) Spouses living together

There is no charge to capital gains tax on a transfer of assets between husband and wife provided that they have been living together in the year of assessment in which the transfer takes place (Taxation of Chargeable Gains Act 1992) ('TCGA 1992'), s 58. This continues to apply notwithstanding the introduction of independent taxation from 6 April 1990. Usually a husband and wife are regarded as living together if they are not separated under a court order or a deed of separation or separated in such circumstances as are likely to prove permanent (Income and Corporation Taxes Act 1988, s 282). The Revenue treat the separation as likely to be permanent if the parties have been living apart for one year (*Pinson on Revenue Law*, 17th edn, para 38–04).

In many cases the husband and wife will be living apart at the time of the court order, or at a time when agreement is reached between them concerning the former matrimonial home, in circumstances that are likely to prove permanent. Indeed the parties may in any event no longer be husband and wife. *Prima facie*, therefore, a charge to capital gains tax will arise on any transfer by the husband to the wife of the former matrimonial home or of his share or interest in it.

(b) Only or main residence

Relief from any liability to capital gains tax on any transfer should be available in most cases because the former matrimonial home will have been the only or main residence of both the husband and the wife. Section 222 of the TCGA 1992, provides that gains accruing on the disposal of, or an interest in, a dwelling house which is or has been an individual's only or main residence (together with garden or grounds of up to half a hectare in extent or other extent appropriate for the reasonable enjoyment of the residence according to the size and character of the dwelling house) throughout the period of ownership (but disregarding the last 36 months of that period (TCGA 1992, s 223) are exempt from capital gains tax. As to the inclusion of other properties (eg a gardener's cottage) within the exemption see *Lewis v Rook* [1992] 1 WLR 662.

It is clear therefore that a sale of the former matrimonial home within 36 months of the husband leaving it, or a transfer of his interest in it to the wife within that period, will not incur any charge to capital gains tax.

It will be otherwise if a sale or transfer takes place when the husband left the home at least 36 months ago or the husband has acquired another residence. In this case, only a proportion of the gain will be exempt by reference to the period of actual occupation and to the last 36 months of ownership. The balance will be subject to capital gains tax. As an example, if there is a gain on the sale of a property owned equally for fifteen years, occupied for the first ten years by both husband and wife and for the last five years by only the wife, there is complete exemption on the one-half share occupied by the wife throughout, and a chargeable gain to the extent of two-fifteenths of the gain on the other half (the chargeable years being the five years after occupation had ceased less the 36 months). This brings us to consideration of the extra-statutory concession.

(c) Extra-statutory concession D6

This concession happily can exempt the whole gain resulting from the disposal from a charge to capital gains tax even if the conveyance or transfer to the wife takes place 36 months after the husband has left the former matrimonial home. It is quoted in full:

6 *Private residence exception: separated couples*

Where a married couple separate or are divorced and one partner ceases to occupy the matrimonial home and subsequently as part of a financial settlement disposes of the home, or an interest in it, to the other partner the home may be regarded for the purposes of Sections [222 to 224 of TCGA 1992] 101 to 103 as continuing to be a residence of the transferring partner from the date his or her occupation ceases until the date of transfer, provided that it has throughout this period been the other partner's only or main residence. Thus, where a husband leaves the matrimonial home while still owning it, the usual capital gains tax exemption or relief for a taxpayer's only or main residence would be given on the subsequent transfer to the wife, provided she has continued to live in the house and the husband has not elected that some other house should be treated for capital gains tax purposes as his main residence for this period.

The wording of the concession would seem to suggest that if the husband moves out of the matrimonial home and makes no election that his new home is his main residence then he need do nothing further, since on any subsequent transfer of the former matrimonial home to his former wife the principal private dwelling house exemption will be available (provided she has continued to live there).

The Revenue are of the view that a taxpayer's home (even if a rented flat) can be his main residence even if he does not own it. If a taxpayer has two residences he can elect which of them is to be treated as his main residence (s 222(5)) for the purpose of the exemption and notwithstanding the terms of the above concession the husband can avoid difficulty if he makes a positive election.

If the husband elects that his 'new' home is to be treated as his main residence, then the disposal to the wife of the former matrimonial home (or his interest in it) will give rise to a charge to capital gains tax; this will be on the gain accruing in respect of the period from when the matrimonial home ceased to be his main residence until the date of the court order or date of agreement between the parties. Section 222(5)(*a*) contains a time-limit of two

years during which the election as to main residence can be made
and if an election is not made within the period the question of
which is the main residence is determined by the Inspector of
Taxes, subject to the usual right of appeal. By making a positive
election the husband avoids the Inspector making a determination
under s 222(5)(*b*) as to which is the husband's main residence and
avoids the necessity for an appeal and having to claim the benefit
of the concession. In practice a great deal of discretion is exercised
by the Revenue with regard to this section, but to avoid an
unexpected tax liability in relation to the transfer by the husband
of the former matrimonial home to the wife the husband is well
advised to consider making his election within the two-year
period.

A cautionary note should be added: the separated wife may be
in possession of the fomer matrimonial home and wish to move
house. If she does so and the husband purchases the replacement
house for her, and she occupies it on the same terms, a subsequent
transfer to her of that house will not be within the terms of the
concession (see p 18) because that house will never have been a
matrimonial home. A charge to capital gains tax could therefore
arise unless the provisions of the TCGA 1992, s 225, apply (as to
which see Chapter 6, p 100).

(d) Other reliefs

The above has been concerned with the only or main residence or
the husband's interest therein being transferred absolutely to the
wife. A transfer of other real property, such as the holiday home
to the wife, will give rise to a capital gains liability if at the time of
the transfer, as is more than likely, the parties are separated in
such circumstances as are likely to prove permanent or are
separated under a court order (see p 16) (see, for example,
Aspden v Hildesley [1982] 1 WLR 264 where a transfer of property
which had never been the husband's main residence was made to
the wife six years after the parties separated). Assuming that a
capital gains tax liability is likely to arise, *prima facie* this will fall
upon the husband as the conveying party or transferor; this
potential liability should be taken into account, but regard should
be had to other reliefs:

(i) *'Hold-over' relief*—Since the restriction of this relief by
the Finance Act 1989, s 124 it is only likely to be

available in business property transfer situations (such as a guest house or nursing home) (see TCGA 1992, s 165). The potential liability would pass to the wife as transferee; to agree to elect for 'hold over' cannot necessarily be to her advantage.

(ii) *Annual exemption*—This is £5,800 in the tax year 1992/93 (TCGA 1992, s 3 and Capital Gains Tax (Annual Exempt Amount) Order 1992 (SI No 626)).

(iii) *Indexation allowance*—As from 31 March 1982 or later acquisition date, the acquisition cost of the matrimonial home is to be increased in line with the Retail Prices Index (TCGA 1992, s 53).

The potential liability where the former matrimonial home is settled upon certain trusts is considered in Chapter 6.

3 Inheritance tax

If both husband and wife are domiciled in the United Kingdom, any transfer of assets between them is exempt from any charge to inheritance tax (Inheritance Tax Act 1984, s 18(1) formerly the Capital Transfer Tax Act 1984). Further, a disposition between the separated spouses will rank as a transfer between the spouses; so that the exemption is still available, as there is no requirement (in contrast to the capital gains tax legislation—see p 16) that the spouses shall be living together.

Thus, as long as the marriage between the husband and wife (assuming them both to be domiciled in the UK) is not dissolved, transfer of property between them will not incur a liability to inheritance tax. The marriage is not finally dissolved until the decree is made absolute; thus, transfers of property in the period between the decree nisi and the decree absolute from husband to wife incur no inheritance tax liability.

Once the marriage is dissolved, *prima facie* there is a charge to inheritance tax on a transfer of property between husband and wife unless the disposition is *not* intended to confer gratuitous benefit on either person and is made between persons not connected with each other (Inheritance Tax Act 1984, s 10(1)). A former husband and wife are not 'connected persons' (see TCGA 1992, s 286(2), and Inheritance Tax Act 1984, s 270).

It will be recalled that all transfers of property ordered by the court take effect only after the decree absolute (Matrimonial Causes Act 1973, s 24(3)), at which time the exemption relating to a transfer between husband and wife is not applicable. In most cases, however, a transfer of property from the former husband to the former wife will fall within the provisions of s 10(1) mentioned above and the Inland Revenue have issued a Press Statement (see *Orange Tax Handbook* 1992/93, Butterworths, IHT Statements of Practice, E12) to this effect:

> Transfer of money or property pursuant to an Order of the Court in consequence of a Decree of Divorce or nullity of marriage will in general be regarded as exempt from Inheritance Tax as transactions at arm's length which are not intended to confer any gratuitous benefit.

If it can be shown, therefore, that a transfer of property takes place to satisfy the claim of the former wife (ie that there is no gratuitous benefit intended) there should be no charge on the transfer to inheritance tax. Similarly if the house is transferred upon certain terms and conditions (see Chapter 6) s 11 of the Inheritance Tax Act 1984 should relieve the transfer from charge (see p 99) on the basis that it is for the maintenance of the other party to the marriage. The safest course, in view of the Revenue's Statement, must be either to complete the transfer (if by agreement) before the marriage is dissolved or to have the transfer made the subject of a court order and so usually fall within the provisions of s 10(1).

A sale by a former husband to the former wife of property or his interest therein should incur no inheritance tax liability if at full value, but if a sale takes place at an under value on the basis that a benefit is intended this is a transfer of value for inheritance tax purposes. Following the Finance Act 1986 this would be a potentially exempt transfer and only subject to a charge to inheritance tax if the husband transferor dies within seven years of the date of the transfer (Finance Act 1986, Sched 19, Pt I, para 1 inserting s 3(A) Inheritance Tax Act 1984).

In the event of the death of the husband within the seven year period, the liability to inheritance tax falls upon the transferee wife (Inheritance Tax Act 1984, s 199) although if not paid within 12 months the husband's personal representatives can be liable (s 199(2)). The husband should take an indemnity from the wife to protect his estate in the event of such liability arising.

4 Stamp duty

It is often forgotten why it is necessary to stamp conveyances or transfers with stamp duty. Section 14(4) of the Stamp Act 1891, in effect provides that an instrument not sufficiently stamped shall not be available as evidence in any civil proceedings. Thus, in unregistered conveyancing unless a conveyance or other document of title is properly stamped, it cannot be used to assert title to land or defend that title if attacked by others. For this reason any purchaser will wish to see that all documents in the chain of title are properly stamped.

In respect of registered land, a transferee will not be concerned with the amount of stamp duty imposed on documents prior to the transfer to him; the registrar is under a duty to check the sufficiency of the stamping on a document affecting registered land (Stamp Act 1891, s 17), so that an instrument cannot be registered at HM Land Registry unless correctly stamped.

Section 12 of the Stamp Act 1891 allows any person to submit a document for adjudication to the Adjudication Section of the Inland Revenue Stamp Office. If there is doubt, therefore, as to whether or not a document should be stamped, and if so with what duty, the safest course is to submit it for adjudication. The executed document, together with a plain copy of it, must be submitted. Adjudication is generally conclusive as to the sufficiency of the stamp duty, so that objection cannot be taken either in court proceedings or by any purchaser (Stamp Act 1891, s 12(5)).

In the case of a conveyance on sale (or assignment of a lease by way of sale) a 'PD' stamp is necessary as well, to show that particulars of the transaction have been delivered to the Inland Revenue (Finance Act 1931, s 28).

(a) The reliefs

Section 83 of the Finance Act 1985 made very significant changes to the stamping of documents executed on or after 26 March 1985 where property is conveyed or transferred from one party to a marriage to the other. The section relates to any instrument that:

> (i) is executed in pursuance of an order of a court made on granting in respect of the parties a decree of divorce, nullity of marriage or judicial separation, or

(ii) is executed in pursuance of an order of a court which is made in connection with the dissolution or annulment of the marriage or the parties' judicial separation and which is made at any time after the granting of such a decree, or

(iii) is executed at any time in pursuance of an agreement of the parties made in contemplation of or otherwise in connection with the dissolution or annulment of the marriage or their judicial separation.

The section specified that stamp duty of 50p was payable on such an instrument.

Even that can be avoided following the coming into force on 1 May 1987 of The Stamp Duty (Exempt Instruments) Regulations 1987 (SI No 516). These provide that if the appropriate certificate is included as part of the instrument or is endorsed thereon, then no stamp duty is payable. The certificate must be signed by the transferor (which it will be if included in the conveyance/transfer) or by his solicitors or duly authorised agent.

Category H of the Regulations relates to:

> The conveyance or transfer of property within section 83(1) of the Finance Act 1985 (transfers in connection with divorce etc).

Thus, in general, most 'matrimonial conveyances' should not incur any liability to stamp duty whatever the value of the property conveyed or transferred.

(b) Assuming the mortgage debt

In the past practitioners have had considerable difficulty where the transferee wife took over property subject to a mortgage liability. *Prima facie*, this raised a liability to stamp duty under s 57 of the Stamp Act 1891 according to the value of the debt assumed by the transferee. The Inland Revenue has now clarified the position (Statement of Practice SP6/90 dated 27 April 1990):

(i) this section does not affect conveyances or transfers which fall within s 83 of the Finance Act 1985 and Category H above;

(ii) if on a conveyance or transfer of property subject to a debt (not within the provisions of s 83) the transferee covenants (either in the instrument or separately) to pay the debt or indemnify the transferor in respect thereof such covenant constitutes valuable consideration and establishes the transaction as a sale for stamp duty purposes.

Where no express covenant is given by the transferee, the Revenue takes the view that one is implied unless a contrary intention is shown (and may always be implied where property was previously in joint names with both parties jointly liable on the mortgage).

Thus, unless s 83 above applies, a mortgaged property transferred from one spouse to another or into joint names will incur a charge to stamp duty unless it is clear that the transferor alone remains liable for the debt. Similarly, a transfer of mortgaged property from joint names to one name alone is likely to incur a liability for stamp duty, although the Revenue's practice would be to charge duty on the proportion of debt assumed by the transferee (usually one half).

In a non husband and wife situation (ie where no other reliefs are available) the mortgage debt assumed will be added to the consideration paid to arrive at the total amount subject to stamp duty.

(c) The charge

If the conveyance or transfer does not fall within the provisions of s 83, one is thrown back on the previous stamp duty position:

(i) *conveyance or transfer on sale* This incurs a charge to *ad valorem* stamp duty at 1 per cent unless the conveyance can be certified at £60,000 or less (see below) (Finance Act 1984, s 109 and Finance Act 1993); or

(ii) *conveyance or transfer 'of any other kind'* In such a case fixed stamp duty of 50p is payable unless the instrument can be certified as being one within The Stamp Duty (Exempt Instruments) Regulations 1987 (SI No 516).

(d) The hybrid situation

It is sometimes agreed between the parties to a marriage that the matrimonial home (or the husband's interest therein) be transferred to the wife and a third party (eg a new husband—see Chapter 5). This is, in essence, a truncation of two separate transactions (a transfer to the wife followed by her subsequent transfer to herself and the third party) each of which could be the subject of a certificate under The Stamp Duty (Exempt Instruments) Regulations 1987 (SI No 516) (Categories H and L respectively). However, the truncated conveyance would not then be 'an instrument by which property is conveyed or transferred from one party to a marriage to the other' within the Finance Act 1985, s 83 and therefore could not be certified by the husband as being within category 'H' of the Regulations. The situation would therefore be as set out in section (c) above and adjudication is advised.

(e) Examples

Set out below are various categories of conveyance/transfers and how they should be dealt with for stamp duty purposes:

(i) *Conveyance or transfer pursuant to court order — no monetary consideration*

(Eg Precedents 1, 2, 7, 8, 15 and 16)
Provided this contains the following certificate (it is suggested as part of the instrument) no stamp duty is payable. Adjudication is not necessary:

> It is certified that this instrument falls within category H in the Schedule to The Stamp Duty (Exempt Instruments) Regulations 1987.

(ii) *Conveyance or transfer by the husband to the wife, by agreement (ie not pursuant to court order) — no monetary consideration*

Provided this meets the requirements of the Finance Act 1985, s 83(1)(c) (see above) and provided the certificate in (i) above is contained in the instrument, no stamp duty is payable. Adjudication is not necessary.

(iii) *Conveyance or transfer pursuant to court order or by agreement — wife paying some consideration to husband*

(Eg Precedents 56 and 57)
If by order of the court (or by agreement) and within the

provisions of s 83 (above) then provided the certificate in (i) above is contained in the instrument, no stamp duty is payable. Adjudication is not necessary.

   (iv) *Conveyance or transfer pursuant to court order with husband being released from the mortgage (wife assuming liability)*

(Eg Precedents 5, 6, 19 and 20)
It was this type of conveyance which caused the most difficulty prior to the passing of the Finance Act 1985 because the Stamp Act 1891, s 57 triggered a charge to stamp duty (see above). Happily, such a conveyance falls within the provisions of s 83 (above) and with the addition of the exemption certificate (see (i) above) no charge to stamp duty arises.

   (v) *Conveyance or transfer by husband to wife (or a third party) for consideration (no element of gift)*

(Eg Precedents 9, 10, 17, 18, 34 to 39)
Such a conveyance if not falling within the provisions of s 83 (above) (ie not made in connection with the divorce) and not containing an element of gift requires the conventional stamp duty certificate, if the consideration is under £60,000.

> It is hereby certified that the transaction hereby effected does not form part of a larger transaction or of a series of transactions in respect of which the amount or value or the aggregate amount or value of the consideration exceeds £60,000.

If the consideration is in excess of this figure, then no certificate is required and *ad valorem* stamp duty at the rate of 1 per cent of the consideration will be payable.

   It must not be forgotten that if the wife or third party is assuming the mortgage debt, so that the husband is released, the amount of the debt assumed in addition to the cash consideration will be subject to stamp duty (Stamp Act 1891, s 57).

(vi) *Conveyance or transfer by husband to wife, not within s 83, with element of gift—no monetary consideration*

Although hardly within the circumstances mentioned in this book, such a conveyance does avoid a charge to stamp duty by virtue of the Regulations and provided that it is a conveyance or transfer of property operating as a voluntary disposition inter vivos for no consideration in money or money's worth nor any consideration referred to in s 57 of the Stamp Act 1891 (conveyance in consideration of a debt etc). The certificate to be contained in the instrument would be:

> It is certified that this instrument falls within category L in The Schedule to The Stamp Duty (Exempt Instruments) Regulations 1987

The instrument so certified does not require adjudication.

(vii) *Conveyance or transfer to trustees (by Court order or by agreement) with no consideration*

(Eg Precedents 46 to 49)
Such a conveyance or transfer falls outside the provisions of s 83 (above) as it is not a conveyance or transfer from one party to a marriage to the other. Certificate H is not applicable.

Although the document creates a settlement (see p 99) Certificate L is not applicable because it is not a voluntary disposition. The document will thus be a conveyance or transfer 'of any other kind' (see p 24) and stamp duty of 50p is payable; practitioners may prefer to submit the document to the Inland Revenue Adjudication Section.

Chapter 3

Home in Husband's Name — Conveyance to Wife

This chapter deals with the situation where the matrimonial home is in the sole name of the husband, with the home being either free from any mortgage charge or subject to a mortgage debt. The court may order the husband to convey or transfer the home to the wife absolutely in the following manner:

> It is ordered that the Respondent shall transfer as beneficial owner to the Petitioner absolutely within 28 days from the date of this Order the property at 1 Blackacre Drive, Blackacre.

Chapter 6 deals with those cases where the home is in the husband's sole name and the husband is ordered to make a conveyance upon certain terms or settle the matrimonial home upon certain trusts.

The risk of the husband dealing with the property in the period between the court order and completion of the conveyance to the wife or lodgment of the transfer to her at HM Land Registry has already been mentioned (see above p 10) and practitioners will no doubt have taken protective steps accordingly.

1 Procedure

As the house is in the husband's sole name, the husband's solicitors will have possession of the title deeds unless there is a mortgage. If there is a bank or building society mortgage the husband's solicitors should be able to obtain the title deeds from the mortgagee.

Some solicitors acting for the husband may take a robust view to save their clients costs and, following the court order, may merely dispatch the title deeds to the wife's solicitors on the basis that the husband has no further interest in them and that they will receive a conveyance for execution by the husband in due course. In unregistered conveyancing this is not satisfactory, as the husband's solicitors cannot (unless they have taken an abstract) check on receiving the conveyance for execution if proper indemnities are proferred in respect of any covenants and other matters to which the property is subject. It is considered more satisfactory to adhere to the conventional conveyancing procedure so that the husband's solicitors will submit an epitome of title to the wife's solicitors or (in the case of registered land) office copy entries of the registered title. Obtaining office copy entries (as opposed to furnishing merely a copy of the registered title) is advisable as it reveals at an early stage whether or not there is a second charge which may not have been disclosed to the husband's solicitors.

In the case of a matrimonial home which does not have registered title, it would seem to be accepted practice to assume that the title was properly investigated at the time of the husband's purchase, so that all the husband's solicitors need to abstract to the wife's solicitors is the conveyance to the husband, any mortgage, any 'sales-off' (or other transactions affecting the title), and details of the covenants affecting the property.

Following the receipt of the epitome of title or office copy entries, the wife's solicitors will submit a draft conveyance or transfer to the husband's solicitors and engross the same after approval. Although the court order should specify a time-limit in which the conveyance must be completed (so that compliance can be enforced—see Chapter 8) such time-limit is rarely adhered to in practice. There can be no incentive for an embittered husband to execute the conveyance quickly. If a more than reasonable time has elapsed since the engrossed conveyance or transfer was submitted for execution by the husband, then the steps set out in Chapter 8 are a guide as to the procedure to be followed before application is made to the court asking the court to execute the conveyance or transfer on behalf of the husband.

For the reason that there can so often be delay in obtaining the husband's signature, it is recommended that only once the documentation has been agreed and executed should a 'completion date' be arranged so that the wife's solicitors can make the

necessary searches against the husband in HM Land Charges
Registry or HM Land Registry (as the case may be). In the latter
case (unless the wife is purchasing the property or the mortgagee
is advancing monies when the ordinary search Form 94A is
appropriate) a search on Form 94C should be made, although
such a search does not confer priority for the registration of any
dealing (Land Registration (Official Searches) Rules 1990 (SI No
1361), r 9) and in contrast to Form 94A requires a fee of £8 (Land
Registration Fees Order 1992). If the property is being charged by
way of mortgage by the wife then priority can be obtained by the
mortgagee's solicitors making the usual Form 94A Search on
behalf of the mortgagee, which gives a priority period of 30
working days (Land Registration (Official Searches) Rules 1990
(SI No 1361), r 3).

2 Covenants for title

(a) Unregistered land

The question as to what covenants for title should be implied in
the conveyance may be in issue. Clearly, if the court orders the
conveyance, or if the conveyance is by agreement to satisfy the
claim of the wife, it will be inappropriate for the husband to
convey 'as settlor' since the conveyance is not a voluntary
disposition or settlement; for this to be an effective covenant the
conveying party must not only be expressed to convey as 'settlor',
he must actually be a settlor (see *Fay v Miller Wilkins & Co* [1941]
Ch 360, although *Emmet on Title* (19th edn, Longman, para
14.003) expresses doubts concerning this decision).

It is tempting to adopt the view that the husband should convey
'as trustee', thus implying that he himself has not incumbered the
property (see Law of Property Act 1925, s 76(1)(F), Sched 2, Pt
VI). Section 76(1)(F) 'LPA 1925', specifies that the covenant set
out in Sched 2, Pt VI, is implied when the conveyance is made
under an order of the court. Few standard conveyancing text-
books mention, let alone discuss, the covenant implied in a
conveyance made under 'an order of the court' and there is a sug-
gestion by reason of the heading to Part VI that such a covenant
is only to be used where the court orders a conveyance on behalf
of a person suffering under a disability.

One is led to the conclusion therefore that the husband should convey as beneficial owner; he is very often conveying the former matrimonial home as part of an agreement whereby the wife releases her rights to further claims for capital, and as such he could be said to be receiving valuable consideration from her and it is established that a vendor selling under compulsion should stand in the same position as a contractual purchaser under an open contract (see *Re King* [1962] 1 WLR 632 and *Emmet on Title* above).

If the wife was a purchaser for money, she would insist on the husband conveying as 'beneficial owner', and there seems no good reason therefore why she should not receive the benefit of these implied covenants when taking a conveyance of the matrimonial home from the husband by order of the court or by way of final agreement between them. It is, therefore, recommended that such covenant be insisted upon.

It may be helpful to recall that the 'beneficial owner' covenants imply:

(i) *Full power to convey* – the vendor has a good right to convey the whole property and interest agreed to be conveyed.

(ii) *Quiet enjoyment* – the purchaser shall have quiet enjoyment of the land.

(iii) *Freedom from incumbrances* – the land shall be enjoyed free from any incumbrances other than those subject to which the conveyance is expressly made.

(iv) *Further assurance* – the vendor will execute such assurances and do such things as are necessary to cure any defect in the conveyance.

As the 'beneficial owner' covenants are only implied where there is valuable consideration (see LPA 1925, s 76(1)(*a*)) Clause 2 set out in Precedent 1 below should be expressly incorporated in the conveyance if there is no cash payment.

In an assignment of unregistered leasehold land for valuable consideration a covenant by the assignor as 'beneficial owner' implies (in addition to the freehold beneficial owner covenants) that the lease is valid, that the rent has been paid and the covenants and conditions of the lease have been observed and performed (LPA 1925, s 76(1)(*b*)) with a separate covenant being implied that the assignee will pay the rent, observe and perform

the covenants and conditions in the lease and indemnify the
assignor in respect thereof (LPA 1925, s 77(1)(c)).

Unless there is valuable consideration (as on sale) the beneficial
owner covenants (just as in the case of the conveyance of
freeholds) will have to be expressly incorporated in the assignment. Express mention of the beneficial owner covenants will
imply on the part of the assignor that the terms of the lease with
regard to maintenance, decoration and repair have been complied
with; this may not be so especially if the husband has been absent
from the property for some time (see generally *Butler v Mount-
view Estates* [1951] 2 KB 563). Whilst, *prima facie*, the wife could
sue the husband on this implied covenant if the leasehold
covenants have not been complied with, it is likely (in view of the
fact that she must have known the state and condition of the
property) that the husband could have the assignment rectified to
exclude this covenant; far better therefore, if applicable, to
exclude this part of the beneficial owner covenant *ab initio*. (See
Precedent 3.)

(b) Registered land

In the case of registered land (whether freehold or leasehold) the
wording of r 76 of the Land Registration Rules 1925 (SR & O 1925
No 1093) suggests that if the husband is expressed to convey as
'beneficial owner' (whether or not there is any consideration)
these covenants for title will be implied. The position cannot be
regarded as free from doubt and it is therefore recommended that
the express provision set out in Precedent 2 be incorporated in the
transfer.

A transfer of registered land made otherwise than for valuable
consideration is subject to all minor interests (see Land Registration Act 1925, ss 20(4) and 23(5)); the taking of the express
'beneficial owner' covenants gives the wife the additional protection that if in fact the property is subject to any claim or demand
not previously revealed, not only would any right of action in
respect thereof against the husband be better founded, but the
implied covenant for further assurance (implied in the beneficial
owner covenants but not in the covenant as 'trustee') will require
the husband to execute and do all assurances and things necessary
for further assuring the subject matter of the transfer. (See
Dunning v Sykes [1987] Ch 287 and Ruoff and Roper, *Registered
Conveyancing* Looseleaf edn, Sweet and Maxwell, 1991, £16.05).

It will be appreciated that no reference to the implied covenants will appear on the register (see r 76). Should any question arise, however, the Registrar has a discretion (under Land Registration Rules 1925, r 290(1)) to allow inspection of the filed transfer and it is understood that such discretion would be exercised if any difficulty could be resolved by production of the filed transfer.

In respect of registered leaseholds s 24 of the Land Registration Act 1925 implies on a transfer similar covenants to those in unregistered conveyancing, namely that the transferor has paid the rent and observed and performed the covenants of the lease and that the transferee will pay future rent, observe and perform the leasehold covenants and keep the transferor indemnified in respect thereof.

In order that the transferor be relieved from liability in respect of lack of repair prior to the transfer (see p 32) express mention to that effect should be made in the transfer, a copy of which might prudently be retained to avoid asking the registrar to exercise his discretion under r 290 above.

3 Where the property is subject to a mortgage

(a) First mortgage only

The court may order that:

> The Respondent shall as beneficial owner transfer to the Petitioner absolutely within 28 days from the date of this Order the property at 1 Blackacre Drive, Blackacre, subject to the existing mortgage in favour of the Blackacre Building Society.

Alternatively, agreement to this effect may be reached between the husband and the wife and embodied in a 'consent' order (as to the advantages of which, see Chapter 1).

In such a case, the husband will, if possible, wish to be released by the mortgagee from the future liability under the mortgage rather than rely upon an indemnity from the wife, and although the mortgagee should be aware of the proceedings between the parties by virtue of the notification required to be made to it under r 2.59(4) of the Family Proceedings Rules 1991 (see p 3), a formal application will doubtless have to be made by the husband for a release. It must be remembered that a court cannot order a mortgagee to agree to a conveyance or transfer subject to mortgage, nor can it order a mortgagee to release a party from the mortgage covenants.

If the wife's level of income is sufficient, the mortgagee will probably consent to the release of the husband from liability under the mortgage so long as the wife covenants to assume this and, depending upon the practice of the mortgagee, will specify what clauses it requires in the appropriate conveyance or transfer. Some mortgagees insist on approving the draft conveyance or transfer and regard must therefore be had to the practice of each mortgagee. The release of the husband from his obligations under the mortgage (as in Precedent 5) will not release him from the covenants for title implied under s 76(1) of the Law of Property Act 1925 by his having charged the property as beneficial owner (*The Conveyancer*, 1982, p 252); this lack of complete release however is necessary for the mortgagee so that it still has the covenant for further assurance in the event that a defect in title becomes apparent and some mortgagees insist on a specific covenant to this effect.

If the mortgagee will not consent to the husband being released from the mortgage, then the husband will have to be content with an indemnity from the wife (see Precedents 7 and 8).

Strictly, as far as unregistered conveyancing is concerned, there is no need for the mortgagee to be a party to the conveyance if it is not releasing the husband from liability. In practice most mortgagees require to join in the conveyance. It is obviously in the husband's interest that the mortgagee receives a covenant from the wife to observe and perform the terms of the mortgage as this will put the mortgagee on further notice as to the primary responsibility notwithstanding that the husband is not released. The exact terms of the covenant to be given should be checked with the mortgagee concerned.

If the title to the matrimonial home is registered, then a consent to the transfer will be required from the mortgagee if a restriction to this effect has been entered on the register.

Owing to the provisions of *Williams & Glyn's Bank Ltd v Boland* and *Williams & Glyn's Bank Ltd v Brown* [1981] AC 487 it would be prudent to obtain the consent to the conveyance from any other occupier of the matrimonial home aged 18 years or more, coupled with confirmation from such occupier that he or she is agreeable to the rights of the mortgagee taking priority over his or her rights in the property or its proceeds of sale. Most building societies have produced standard forms of consent. (See Precedent 11.)

It is suggested that the conveyance be prepared and executed in duplicate so that the husband has a record of the terms of the indemnity given to him by the wife.

As far as registered land is concerned r 110 of the Land Registration Rules 1925 covers the position:

> On a transfer of land subject to a charge or other incumbrance appearing on the register . . . covenants by either party to pay the money owing and to indemnify the other party may be added to the instrument of transfer and may be noted on the register.

Application to this effect should therefore be included in the transfer (see Precedent 8). The entry will be placed on the Proprietorship Register and will read:

> Note: The transfer to the proprietor contains a covenant by her with [*Husband*] to pay the monies secured by Charge No 1 and to indemnify him from all claims and demands in respect thereof.

It is not necessary for the building society to be joined as a party to a registered land transfer where it is only receiving the benefit of a covenant to observe and perform the terms of the mortgage by the wife (and not releasing the husband) because it can enforce the covenant without being a party (*Chelsea and Walham Green Building Society v Armstrong* [1951] Ch 853). It is suggested, however, that the building society be joined so that it is specifically aware of the terms of the transfer.

As in unregistered conveyancing it is probably advisable that the husband keeps a duplicate or certified copy of the transfer to the wife so that he has a record of the terms of indemnity given to him by the wife.

(b) Where in addition there is a second charge

If the former matrimonial home to be conveyed or transferred to the wife is subject to both a first and second charge it may be that whilst the first mortgagee is prepared to release the husband, upon having a direct covenant by the wife, the second mortgagee is not so agreeable. It is obviously to the husband's advantage in such circumstances to seek to persuade the first mortgagee to offer the wife a further advance of sufficient amount to repay the second charge. That failing, there can be a conveyance between the husband and wife, to which the first mortgagee is a party, to release the husband from liability under the first mortgage and take a covenant to observe and perform the same from the wife who will also covenant with the husband to indemnify him in respect of the second mortgage. The second mortgagee should also be a party to receive the additional covenant of the wife.

Alternatively, there can be a conveyance between the husband and the wife to which the first mortgagee is a party (as above) and a deed of covenant from the wife in favour of the second mortgagee to observe and perform the terms of the second mortgage, containing an indemnity in favour of the husband in respect thereof.

In the first case, the conveyance should be prepared and executed in triplicate (or there should be examined copies) so that the original is held by the first mortgagee, the husband has a record of the indemnity and release given and the second mortgagee also has a record of the transfer.

In the second case, there will need to be an original and a duplicate (or examined copy) of each document so that the husband has a record of the release from the first mortgage and of the indemnity given him in respect of the second mortgage.

As far as registered conveyancing is concerned, there seems no reason why the transfer should not be prepared and executed in triplicate (or an original with examined copies), the original transfer being lodged at HM Land Registry, the duplicate being held with the second charge certificate and the third being retained by the husband as evidence of his release from the first mortgage and of the indemnity in respect of the second mortgage. Rule 110 of the Land Registration Rules 1925 will be applicable (see p 35).

4 Steps to be taken following completion of the conveyance or transfer

(a) Stamp duty

No 'PD Form' is required unless there has been a conveyance on sale (eg Precedents 9 and 10). If the consideration is less than

£60,000 and the property already has registered title, the PD Form should be sent to HM Land Registry with the application for registration of the transfer. (The Stamp Duty (Exempt Instruments) Regulations 1985 (SI No 1688).)

The precedents in this chapter (with the exception of Precedents 9 and 10 which are not following a court order) should not attract a charge to stamp duty as a result of The Stamp Duty (Exempt Instruments) Regulations 1987 (SI No 516) (see Chapter 2 generally as to stamp duty).

(b) Cancellation at HM Land Charges Registry or Land Registry

No doubt as the matrimonial home was in the husband's sole name the wife will have registered her right of occupation by way of a Class F Land Charge or (if registered title) a notice under the terms of the Matrimonial Homes Act 1983. Although such charge comes to an end by termination of the marriage following the decree absolute, the charge has probably not been cancelled and this should be done at HM Land Charges Registry (Form K13 fee £1) or at HM Land Registry (Form 202 accompanied by a certified copy of the decree absolute—no fee Land Registration Fees Order 1992, Sched 4, Pt II, para (9)).

Any pending action registered at HM Land Charges Registry should be cancelled (Form K11—fee £1.00, Land Charges Fees Rules 1990); any caution registered at HM Land Registry should also be cancelled (Form 71—no fee; para (9) above.

(c) Court order and completion of abstract

It is recommended that a copy of the original court order marked as examined against the original be lodged with the title documents. If the court order refers to matters other than the matrimonial home it is no doubt better to keep these extraneous matters private and to prepare an abstract (and mark the same as examined against the original order) of the relevant part of the court order. A certified copy of the court order (or examined abstract) will be required by HM Land Registry when the transfer is lodged for registration.

Where in registered land a new covenant is given by the wife to the building society a certified copy of the transfer containing the covenant should be lodged with the deeds so that the building society has a proper record there of the wife's liability, the transfer incorporating the covenant itself being retained at the Land Registry.

(d) First registration of title

Although the property may be in an area subject to compulsory registration of title, no application for registration is required when the property is conveyed following a court order as the conveyance has not been one following sale (Land Registration Act 1925, s 123). If the conveyance is one of sale, then registration is compulsory.

(e) HM Land Registry fees

Where the transfer between husband and wife does not involve consideration (eg transfer following agreement between the spouses or pursuant to a court order) then art 2(5) of the Land Registration Fees Order 1992 will apply—fees are based on the value of the land concerned after deducting therefrom the amount secured by any registered charges. Provided the transfer is of the matrimonial home made pursuant to an order of the court, advantage can be taken of Abatement 2(i). Sched 4, Pt I, reducing the fee payable to one-fifth subject to a minimum of £40.

It is simplest to mention the amount of the mortgage debt in the transfer as is done in Precedents 6, 8 and 10. The solicitor lodging the application may specify the value of the property transferred either by letter or on HM Land Registry Form A4.

Where the transfer between husband and wife is one on sale, the fee is calculated in accordance with Scale A, of the 1992 Fee Order on the amount of the consideration.

(f) Insurance

If the property is free from mortgage, the wife should effect her own insurance cover following completion of the conveyance or transfer to her.

If the property is subject to mortgage and the mortgagee concerned has effected cover, confirmation that the name of the insured has been changed to that of the wife should be obtained from the mortgagee.

(g) *Leasehold*

The requirements of the lease as to registration of any assignment with the lessor should be observed.

*   *   *   *

PRECEDENTS

A—Conveyance of entirety to wife.
No mortgage. By court order

Precedent 1—Unregistered Land

THIS CONVEYANCE is made the   day of   19
BETWEEN (1) [*Husband*] of   ('the Husband') and (2)
[*Wife*] of
('the Wife')

WHEREAS:
(A) By a Conveyance ('the Conveyance') dated   and made
between (1) [*previous vendor*] and (2) the Husband the Property herein described was conveyed to the Husband for an estate in fee simple [subject to the covenants and conditions mentioned in the Conveyance but otherwise] free from incumbrances

[*Note*—*If property not subject to covenants and no reference to previous conveyance required, substitute the following:*
(A) The Husband is seised of the Property herein described and hereby conveyed free from incumbrances]

(B) By an Order of [Deputy] District Judge   in the
         County Court dated   in proceedings
between the Husband and the Wife bearing number   the
Husband was ordered to convey the Property to the Wife for an estate in fee simple

NOW pursuant to the Order THIS DEED WITNESSES:-

1 THE Husband as beneficial owner [*see p 30*] conveys to the Wife ALL THAT *etc* TO HOLD the same to the Wife in fee simple [SUBJECT to the covenants and conditions mentioned in the Conveyance so far as the same are still subsisting and capable of taking effect and affect the Property]

2 THE Husband covenants with the Wife in the terms set out in Part I 2nd Schedule Law of Property Act 1925 [*see p 31*]

[3 THE Wife covenants with the Husband that she will observe and perform the said covenants and conditions and will keep the Husband

c

and his personal representatives effectually indemnified against all losses resulting from their non-observance or breach so far as aforesaid]

[**Note to clause 3**—*This clause is only necessary where the husband entered into the original restrictions affecting the property or, in the conveyance to him, covenanted to observe them. Otherwise, he is not entitled to this indemnity. See Williams on Vendor and Purchaser (4th edn, Sweet and Maxwell, 1936, p 685).*]

4 It is certified that this instrument falls within category H in the Schedule to The Stamp Duty (Exempt Instruments) Regulations 1987

IN WITNESS whereof this deed has been duly executed the day and year before written

SIGNED as a Deed
by the Husband in the presence of:
OR   [**Note**—*If a covenant for indemnity is being taken, substitute the following*]

IN WITNESS whereof this deed has been duly executed the day and year before written

SIGNED as a Deed
by the Husband in the presence of:

SIGNED as a Deed
by the Wife in the presence of:

Precedent 2—Registered Land

[**Note**—*It should be possible to use the HM Land Registry Form 19 adding clause 2 from Precedent 1 and deleting the certificate of value so that the form looks as follows*]

Transfer of Whole (Freehold or Leasehold)
(Rule 98 or 115 Land Registration Rules 1925)

HM LAND REGISTRY
Land Registration Acts 1925 to 1986

County and district
or London borough

Title number

Property

Date   1 Pursuant to an Order of [Deputy] District Judge
          in the   County Court dated   in
proceedings between the Transferor and the Transferee bearing number
     I [*Husband*] of   formerly of   ('the
Transferor') as beneficial owner [*see p 32*] transfer to [*Wife*] of
          ('the Transferee') the land comprised in the title above
mentioned

2 The Transferor covenants with the Transferee in the terms set out in Part I 2nd Schedule Law of Property Act 1925 [*see p 32*]

3 The Transferee covenants with the Transferor that she will observe and perform the covenants and conditions referred to in the Charges Register so far as still subsisting and relating to the Property and will keep the Transferor and his personal representatives effectually indemnified against all losses resulting from their non-observance or breach so far as aforesaid

4 [*Stamp Duty Certificate–Precedent 1, clause 4*]

SIGNED as a Deed
by the Transferor in the presence of:

[**Note**–*If covenant for indemnity given, also add the following*]

SIGNED as a Deed
by the Transferee in the presence of:

B–Assignment of leasehold property to wife. No mortgage. By court order

Precedent 3–Unregistered Land

THIS ASSIGNMENT is made the   day of   19
BETWEEN (1) [*Husband*] of   ('the Husband') and (2)
[*Wife*] of   ('the Wife')

WHEREAS:

(A) By a Lease ('the Lease') dated   and made between (1) *X* and (2) *Y* the property hereinafter described was demised by *X* to *Y* for the term of   years subject to the rent thereby reserved and to the covenants and conditions therein contained

(B) The premises demised by the Lease are now vested in the Husband for the residue of the term granted by the Lease subject as foresaid

(C) By an Order of [Deputy] District Judge   in the County Court dated   in proceedings between the Husband and the Wife bearing number   the Husband was ordered to assign the premises comprised in the Lease to the Wife subject as aforesaid

NOW pursuant to the Order THIS DEED WITNESSES:-

1 The Husband as beneficial owner [*see p 31*] ASSIGNS to the Wife ALL THAT *etc* TO HOLD the same to the Wife for all the residue now unexpired of the term of years granted by the Lease SUBJECT henceforth to the payment of the rent thereby reserved and to the covenants and conditions therein contained and on the part of the lessee to be observed and performed

2 The Husband covenants with the Wife in the terms set out in Part I and Part II 2nd Schedule Law of Property Act 1925 and the Wife covenants with the Husband in the terms set out in Part IX 2nd Schedule Law of Property Act 1925 [but so that the covenants on the part of the Husband expressly incorporated herein shall not apply to this assignment so far as they relate to covenants in the Lease for the repair and decoration of the premises thereby demised] [*see p 32*]

3 [*Stamp Duty Certificate—Precedent 1, clause 4*]

IN WITNESS *etc* [*see p 40*]

Precedent 4—Registered Land
[*As in Precedent 2, HM Land Registry Form 19 can be used with suitable amendments*]
[*Same heading as Precedent 2*]

Date
1 Pursuant to an Order of [Deputy] District Judge   in the
          County Court dated   in proceedings between the
Transferor and the Transferee bearing number   I [*Husband*] of
          formerly of   ('the Transferor') as beneficial
owner [*see p 33*] transfer to [*Wife*] of   ('the Transferee') the
land comprised in the title above mentioned for the residue of the term granted by the registered lease

2 [*Covenant for title (see Precedent 2, clause 2)*]

3 The Transferor and the Transferee covenant with each other in the terms set out in Section 24 Land Registration Act 1925 respectively [but so that the covenants on the part of the Transferor implied by Section 24(1)(*a*) thereof shall not apply to this Transfer so far as they relate to the covenants in the registered lease for the repair and decoration of the premises thereby demised] [*see p 33*]

4 [*Stamp Duty Certificate—Precedent 1, clause 4*]

SIGNED *etc* [*see p 41*]

C—Conveyance of entirety to wife by order of court. Property subject to mortgage. Wife (with mortgagee's agreement) assuming liability. Husband released

Precedent 5—Unregistered Land

THIS CONVEYANCE is made the   day of   19
BETWEEN (1) [*Husband*] of   ('the Husband') (2)
          BUILDING SOCIETY whose Chief Office is at
('the Society') and (3) [*Wife*] of   ('the Wife')

WHEREAS:

(A) [*Seisin of the Husband (see Precedent 1, recital (A))*]

(B) By a Mortgage ('the Mortgage') dated   made between (1) the Husband and (2) the Society the Property was charged to the Society to secure the sum of £

(C) By an Order of [Deputy] District Judge   in the   County Court dated   in proceedings between the Husband and the Wife bearing number   the Husband was ordered to convey the Property to the Wife subject to the Mortgage

(D) The Society has agreed to release the Husband from his obligations under the Mortgage

(E) The sum of £   is now owing to the Society on the security of the Mortgage

NOW pursuant to the Order THIS DEED WITNESSES:-

1 THE Husband as beneficial owner [*p 30*] with the consent of the Society conveys to the Wife ALL THAT *etc* TO HOLD the same to the Wife in fee simple SUBJECT TO the Mortgage and all principal money and interest thereby secured [AND SUBJECT ALSO (*continue as in Precedent 1 if property subject to restrictive covenants etc*)]

2 [*Express covenant for title—Precedent 1, clause 2*]

3 THE Society releases and discharges the Husband from his obligations under the Mortgage

4 THE Wife covenants with the Society that she will pay to the Society all principal money interest costs and other monies due or to become due under or by virtue of the Mortgage and will observe and be bound by the agreements covenants and conditions contained or referred to in the Mortgage

[5 *Covenant for indemnity to Husband if property subject to covenants (see Precedent 1, clause 3)*]

6 [*Stamp Duty Certificate—Precedent 1, clause 4*]

IN WITNESS whereof this deed has been duly executed the day and year before written

SIGNED as a Deed by the Husband in the presence of:

SIGNED as a Deed by the Wife in the presence of:

THE COMMON SEAL of the

Society was hereunto affixed
in the presence of:

OR (for Companies authorised not to use a seal)

SIGNED as a Deed by [Limited Company]
acting by [a director and its secretary
or two directors]   Director
                                                     [Secretary or Director]

Precedent 6—Registered Land

[*HM Land Registry Form 19 is not appropriate; this transfer should be typed separately, following HM Land Registry approved format. It is suggested that the transfer be prepared in duplicate (see p 37).*]

[*Same heading as in Precedent 2*]

Date   1 Pursuant to an Order of [Deputy] District Judge
          in the   County Court dated   in
proceedings between the Transferor and the Transferee bearing number
          I [*Husband*] of   formerly of
('the Transferor') as beneficial owner [*see p 32*] transfer to [*Wife*] of
          ('the Transferee') the land comprised in the title above
mentioned SUBJECT to the Charge ('the Registered Charge') dated
          and registered on   under which there is now
owing the sum of £

2 The   ·   Building Society ('the Society') of
being the registered proprietor of the Registered Charge hereby releases
and discharges the Transferor from all obligations under the Registered
Charge

3 The Transferee covenants with the Society that she will pay to the
Society all principal money interest and costs and other monies due or to
become due under or by virtue of the Registered Charge and will
observe and be bound by the agreements covenants and conditions
contained or referred to in the Registered Charge

4 The Transferor covenants with the Transferee in the terms set out in
Part I Second Schedule Law of Property Act 1925 [*see p 32*]

[5 *Covenant for indemnity if property subject to covenants (see Precedent 2, clause 3)*]

6 [*Stamp Duty Certificate—Precedent 1, clause 4*]

SIGNED as a Deed
by the Transferor in the presence of:

SIGNED as a Deed
by the Transferee in the presence of:

THE COMMON SEAL of the
Society was hereunto affixed
in the presence of:

OR (for Companies authorised not to use a seal)

SIGNED as a Deed by [Limited Company]
acting by [a director and its secretary or two directors]
Director
[Secretary or Director]

D—Conveyance of entirety to wife by order of court. Mortgage. Husband remaining liable. Wife indemnifying

Precedent 7—Unregistered Land

THIS CONVEYANCE is made the   day of   19
BETWEEN (1) [*Husband*] of   ('the Husband') (2)
BUILDING SOCIETY whose Chief Office is at   ('the
Society') and (3) [*Wife*] of   ('the wife')

WHEREAS:

(A) [*Seisin of the husband—Precedent 1, recital (A)*]
(B) [*Recital of the mortgage—Precedent 5, recital (B)*]
(C) [*Recital of court order—Precedent 5, recital (C)*]
(D) [*Recital of mortgage debt—Precedent 5, recital (E)*]

NOW pursuant to the Order THIS DEED WITNESSES:-

1 THE Husband as beneficial owner [*see p 31*] with the consent of the Society CONVEYS to the Wife ALL THAT *etc* TO HOLD the same to the Wife in fee simple SUBJECT to the Mortgage and all principal money and interest thereby secured [AND SUBJECT ALSO (*continue as in Precedent 1, clause 1 if property subject to covenants etc*)]

2 [*Express covenant for title—Precedent 1, clause 2*]

3 [*Wife's covenant with building society—Precedent 5, clause 4*]

4 The Wife covenants with the Husband that with effect from [*date*] she will pay and discharge all principal monies interest costs and other monies secured by or henceforth to become payable under the Mortgage and will comply with the covenants therein and will at all times indemnify and keep indemnified the Husband and his estate and effects against all proceedings costs claims and demands in respect thereof

[5 *Covenant for indemnity if appropriate—Precedent 1, clause 3*]

6 [*Stamp Duty Certificate—Precedent 1, clause 4*]

IN WITNESS *etc* [*see Precedent 5*]

Precedent 8—Registered Land

[*Same heading as in Precedent 2*]

Date   1 Pursuant to an Order of [Deputy] District Judge
            in the   County Court dated   in
proceedings between the Transferor and the Transferee bearing number

I [*Husband*] of   formerly of   ('the
Transferor') as beneficial owner [*see p 32*] transfer to [*Wife*] of
            (the 'Transferee') the land comprised in the title above
mentioned SUBJECT to the Charge ('the Registered Charge') dated
            and registered on   under which there is now
owing the sum of £

2 [*Covenant for title*—*Precedent 6, clause 4*]

3 The Transferee covenants with   Building Society ('the
Society') (being the proprietor of the Registered Charge) that she
[*continue as Precedent 6, clause 3*]

4 The Transferee covenants with the Transferor that with effect from
[*date*] she will pay and discharge all principal monies interest costs and
other monies secured by or henceforth to become payable under the
Registered Charge and will comply with the covenants therein and will at
all times indemnify and keep indemnified the Transferor and his estate
and effects against all proceedings costs claims and demands in respect
thereof AND the Transferor and the Transferee hereby make application to the Registrar (under Rule 110 Land Registration Rules 1925)
to note this covenant on the Register [*see p 35*]

[5 *Covenant for indemnity if appropriate (see Precedent 2, clause 3)*]

6 [*Stamp Duty Certificate*—*Precedent 1, clause 4*]

SIGNED *etc* [*see Precedent 6*]

E—Conveyance of entirety to wife. Sale.
Property subject to first and second mortgages.
Wife assuming liability for the first and husband released.
Husband remaining liable on second

Precedent 9—Unregistered Land

THIS CONVEYANCE is made the   day of   19
BETWEEN   (1)   [*Husband*]   of   ('the   Husband')
(2)   BUILDING SOCIETY whose chief office is at
('the Society') (3) the   BANK LIMITED whose registered office
is situate at   ('the Second Mortgagee') and (4) [*Wife*] of
            ('the Wife')

WHEREAS:

(A) [*Seisin of the husband—Precedent 1, recital (A)*]

(B) [*Recital of the first mortgage—Precedent 5, recital (B)*]

(C) By a Mortgage ('the Second Mortgage') dated   and made between (1) the Husband and (2) the Second Mortgagee the Property was charged to the Second Mortgagee subject to the Mortgage to secure the sum of £

(D) The Husband has agreed with the Wife for the sale to her of the Property and the fee simple thereof subject to the Mortgage and the Second Mortgage but otherwise free from incumbrances at the price of £

(E) The Society has agreed to release the Husband from his obligations under the Mortgage

(F) The sum of £   is now owing to the Society on the security of the Mortgage

(G) The sum of £   is now owing to the Second Mortgagee on the security of the Second Mortgage

NOW pursuant to the agreement and in consideration of the sum of £   paid by the Wife to the Husband (the receipt of which the Husband acknowledges)

THIS CONVEYANCE WITNESSES:-

1 The Husband as beneficial owner [*see p 31*] with the consent of the Society and with the consent of the Second Mortgagee CONVEYS to the Wife ALL THAT *etc* TO HOLD the same to the Wife in fee simple SUBJECT to the Mortgage and all principal money and interest thereby secured and SUBJECT ALSO to the Second Mortgage and all principal money and interest thereby secured [SUBJECT ALSO *(as Precedent 1 if property subject to covenants)*]

2 [*Release to husband by first mortgagee—Precedent 5, clause 3*]

3 [*Wife's covenant with first mortgagee—Precedent 5, clause 4*]

4 THE Wife covenants with the Husband that with effect from [*date*] she will pay and discharge all principal monies interest costs and other monies secured by or henceforth to become payable under the Second Mortgage and will comply with the covenants therein and will at all times indemnify and keep indemnified the Husband and his estate and effects against all proceedings costs claims and demands in respect thereof

5 THE Wife covenants with the Second Mortgagee that she will pay to the Second Mortgagee all principal money interest costs and other monies due or to become due under or by virtue of the Second Mortgage

and will observe and be bound by the agreements covenants and conditions contained or referred to in the Second Mortgage

[6 *Covenant for indemnity if appropriate (see Precedent 1, clause 3)*]

7 [See Chapter 2. Stamp duty. Section 83 Finance Act 1985 may apply—see Precedent 1, Clause 4—but if straightforward sale and release of a debt with the consideration under £60,000:

IT IS HEREBY CERTIFIED that the transaction hereby effected does not form part of a larger transaction or of a series of transactions in respect of which the amount or value or the aggregate amount or value of the consideration exceeds £60,000]

IN WITNESS whereof this deed has been duly executed the day and year before written

SIGNED *etc* [*see Precedent 1—for husband and wife*]

THE COMMON SEAL *etc* [*see Precedent 5—for first and second mortgagees*]

Precedent 10—Registered Land

[*Same heading as Precedent 2*]

Date

1 In consideration of pounds (£   ) the receipt of which is acknowledged I [*Husband*] of   formerly of   ('the Transferor') as beneficial owner transfer to [*Wife*] of   ('the Transferee') the land comprised in the title above mentioned SUBJECT
    i) to the Charge ('the Registered Charge') dated   and registered on   under which there is now owing the sum of £   ii) to the Charge ('the Second Registered Charge') dated   and registered on   under which there is now owing the sum of £

2 [*Release to husband by first mortgagee—Precedent 6, clause 2*]

3 [*Covenant by wife with first mortgagee—Precedent 6, clause 3*]

4 The Transferee covenants with the Transferor that with effect from [*date*] she will pay and discharge all principal monies interest costs and other monies secured by or henceforth to become payable under the Second Registered Charge and will comply with the covenants therein and will at all times indemnify and keep indemnified the Transferor and his estate and effects against all proceedings costs claims and demands in respect thereof AND the Transferor and the Transferee hereby make application to the Registrar (under Rule 110 Land Registration Rules 1925) to note this covenant on the Register [*see p 35*]

5 The Transferee covenants with   Bank Limited ('the Second Mortgagee') being the registered proprietor of the Second

Registered Charge that she will pay to the Second Mortgagee all principal money interest costs and other monies due or to become due under or by virtue of the Second Registered Charge and will observe and be bound by the agreements covenants and conditions contained or referred to in the Second Registered Charge

[6 *Covenant for indemnity if appropriate (see Precedent 2, clause 3)*]

7 [*Certificate of value—Precedent 9, clause 7*]

SIGNED *etc* [*see Precedent 6*]

F—Consent to transfer subject to mortgage by occupier

Precedent 11—Unregistered and Registered Land

The Property

The Lender

The Borrower

The Transferor

The Transferee

I, [*Occupier*]
being a person who is in or may go into occupation of the Property:

1 Consent to the transfer of the Property by the Transferor to the Transferee subject to the existing Mortgage in favour of the Lender

2 Agree that such present or future rights or interests that I may have or acquire in or over the Property shall be postponed and made subject to the rights and interests of the Lender under its Mortgage

3 Undertake that no claim to any such rights and interests shall be made by me against the Lender

4 Confirm that I have been advised that I can take independent legal advice on the effect of this document and confirm that the effect of this form of consent has been explained to me

Date

SIGNED by the Occupier
in the presence of:

Chapter 4

Home in Joint Names—
Conveyance to Wife

This chapter deals with the situation where the matrimonial home is held in the joint names of the husband and the wife, either as beneficial joint tenants or as tenants in common. The home may be subject to a mortgage or free from charge.

The court may order the husband to convey or transfer his interest in the home to the wife absolutely in the following manner:

> It is ordered that the Respondent shall transfer to the Petitioner absolutely within 28 days from the date of this Order all his estate and interest in the property 1 Blackacre Drive, Blackacre [subject to the existing Mortgage to the Blackacre Building Society, the Petitioner indemnifying the Respondent against all claims in respect thereof].

Alternatively agreement may be reached between the husband and wife for some monetary payment so that the husband may keep the house in which case the consent order may be:

> It is ordered that the Respondent shall within 28 days from the date of this Order pay to the Petitioner the sum of £   and
> It is ordered that on receipt of the said sum of £   the Petitioner do transfer all her estate and interest in the property at 1 Blackacre Drive, Blackacre to the Respondent.

Chapter 6 deals with those cases where the husband is ordered to convey or transfer his interest in the matrimonial home upon certain terms or settle the same upon certain trusts.

1 Severance

Dealing with the interest of one party in joint property would be incomplete without mention of the doctrine of severance.

Just as solicitors acting for the wife, where the matrimonial home stands in the husband's sole name, will have given advice concerning the registration of a Class F Land Charge or a notice (if registered land); so, where the home stands in the joint names of husband and wife as beneficial joint tenants, will they have advised on severance of that joint tenancy in order to prevent the husband acquiring the whole property by operation of law in the event of the wife's death before the determination of the matrimonial proceedings (see *Barton v Morris* [1985] 2 All ER 1032). The husband's advisers will also have regard to the advantages of severance whilst matrimonial proceedings are pending.

If severance of the joint tenancy takes place, it should be coupled with the making of a new will by the party severing the joint tenancy to deal with 'the severed share'. Although such will does not defeat the claim of the other spouse under the provisions of the Inheritance (Provision for Family and Dependants) Act 1975, if reasonable provision is not made for that spouse, it might be of 'persuasive' use to the court in proceedings under that Act in deciding whether or not to award the surviving spouse a limited interest (eg until remarriage) or an absolute interest in the deceased's share of the matrimonial home.

It was previously thought that severance, where no shares are agreed, operated to create a tenancy in common in equal shares (see Megarry and Wade, *Real Property* 5th edn, Stevens, 1984, p 430 and *R v Porter* [1990] 1 WLR 1260 where the Court of Appeal held that in a joint venture, in the absence of any evidence, the Court was entitled to assume equal sharing). *Goodman v Gallant* [1986] 1 All ER 311 held that in the absence of any claim for rectification or rescission of the original conveyance, evidence could not be subsequently given in support of an unequal divison following severance.

However *Springette v Defoe* [1992] Fam Law 459 (which was not a case between husband and wife) decided that where there had been no discussion between the parties about their respective beneficial interests, the Court could not infer an intention of equal shares; the shares were presumed to be in proportion to their respective contributions. The Court would have to determine the shares (see *Gissing v Gissing* [1971] AC 886). In the light of this it seems that severance is beneficial in that it stops one party acquiring the whole property in the event of the other's death, but the actual shares of the parties would have to await determination by the Court (or agreement).

The procedure for severance differs depending upon whether title to the matrimonial home is registered or not.

(a) Unregistered land

Section 36(2) of the Law of Property Act 1925 provides for severance of a joint tenancy either by:

    (i) a notice in writing given by one joint tenant to the other; or

    (ii) the doing of such other acts or things as would, in the case of personal estate, have been effectual to sever the tenancy in equity.

The mere issue of matrimonial proceedings for a property adjustment order does not automatically sever a joint tenancy (*Harris v Goddard* [1983] 1 WLR 1203) but the issue of proceedings under s 17 of the Married Women's Property Act 1882 can cause severance to occur (*Re Draper's Conveyance* [1969] 1 Ch 486) as does the bankruptcy of one of the parties (*Re Gorman* (a bankrupt) [1990] 1 WLR 616).

The husband and wife may agree that the joint tenancy should be severed but if so they should properly evidence that fact. In *Nielson-Jones v Fedden* [1975] Ch 222 it was held that it was not sufficient for the husband and wife to sign a memorandum to the effect that the husband was to have a free hand to sell the property and use the money to buy a new house for himself although in *Burgess v Rawnsley* [1975] Ch 429 it was held that a beneficial joint tenancy was severed by the oral agreement of one joint tenant to sell her share in the property to the other even though that agreement was not specifically enforceable.

Service of a notice of severance (see Precedent 12) would appear to be effective to sever the joint tenancy if properly addressed to the other joint tenant and received at the property concerned.

It would appear not to matter that the party to whom the notice is addressed does not acknowledge receipt nor even if the party addressed never actually receives the notice itself (see *Re 88 Berkeley Road, London NW9; Rickwood v Turnsek* [1971] Ch 648, and generally as to methods of severance, *Conveyancer NS*, 1976, vol 40, p 77).

If the joint tenancy is severed by agreement then the notice of severance or declaration of trust which would have the same effect (see precedent in *Kelly's Draftsman*, 15th edn, *Butterworths*, 1986, p 673) should specify in what proportions or shares the equitable interests of the former beneficial joint tenants are to be held. If however the shares of each party have never been determined, then at least proper service of the notice of severance ensures that severance has taken place with the advantage as mentioned earlier (see p 51).

Whilst the notice itself may be sufficient to sever the beneficial joint tenancy, to prevent a conveyance by the survivor either through ignorance or fraud it would be prudent to endorse a memorandum on the last conveyance to the effect that severance has taken place. This should be sufficient to put a purchaser on notice so that he insists on paying the purchase monies to two trustees or a trust corporation so as to obtain a good receipt (Law of Property Act 1925, s 27). In the absence of such memorandum or the registration of a petition or receiving order in bankruptcy against any of the joint tenants in HM Land Charges Registry, a purchaser of the legal estate is entitled to treat the survivor as solely and beneficially interested if that survivor is expressed to convey a beneficial owner or if the conveyance includes a statement that such survivor is solely and beneficially interested in the legal estate (Law of Property (Joint Tenants) Act 1964).

(b) Registered land

The position in relation to registered land, while workable, is not wholly satisfactory. Section 74 of the Land Registration Act 1925 provides that, as far as possible, references to trusts shall be excluded from the register. A notice of severance or declaration of trust whilst being effective in equity, would have no effect on the register unless it was completed by an application to register a restriction so that the register shows that the survivor of the former two joint tenants is no longer able to give a valid receipt for capital monies (see Precedent 14). Such application (because the property is registered in the joint names of the husband and wife) requires the signatures of both husband and wife and the submission of the land certificate to the registry. Application will be in Form 75 as required by the Land Registry Rules 1925 (SR & O 1925 No 1093), r 235 (see Precedent 14). Severance results in the obligatory entry of a Form 62 restriction under Land Registration Act 1925, s 63; such Registration incurs no fee (Land Registration Fees Order 1992 (SI No 2089).

If, however, one of the joint proprietors refuses to join in the application to register a restriction, the party giving the notice should apply to HM Land Registry for a restriction to be entered on the basis of his application alone (see *Key and Elphinstone's Precedents in Conveyancing*, 15th edn, Sweet and Maxwell, 1954, vol 3, p 264) again using Form 75. The registrar will probably require to be satisfied that severance has actually taken place. In the writer's experience it will be sufficient to lodge with the application:

> (i) an explanation as to why the application has not been signed by both proprietors (eg the parties are separated and the husband refuses to reply);
>
> (ii) a copy of the notice of severance; and
>
> (iii) a certificate of posting of the notice and confirmation of delivery.

If the other joint tenant has refused to join in an application to register a restriction then doubtless also there will be difficulty about lodging the land certificate. If in fact a charge is already registered then as the land certificate is already notionally deposited at the registry no difficulty would appear to occur and registration can take place.

Where no charge is registered, the registrar, if otherwise prepared to accept the application, may well be prepared to register the restriction without the land certificate provided he is satisfied that severance has taken place (see Ruoff and Roper, *Registered Conveyancing*, Looseleaf edn, Sweet and Maxwell, 1991, §39.21).

It will be appreciated that the registration of a restriction does not specify the shares in which the net proceeds of sale of the property are to be held; so (if agreement) there should be a document (such as a declaration of trust) specifying those shares. However, registration of a restriction protects the share of any deceased former joint tenant whilst the future of the matrimonial home is being clarified.

2 Procedure

Neither the husband nor the wife is solely entitled to hold the title deeds to the matrimonial home in joint names; but, if either party does hold the title deeds, then that party does, of course, hold them as trustee for both the husband and the wife.

Assuming that the husband will be the conveying party or transferor, it would seem appropriate that his solicitors should be allowed custody of the title deeds and act, in effect, as the 'vendor's solicitors'. It is felt that the conventional conveyancing procedure should be adhered to for the reasons stated in Chapter 3.

As the property was purchased jointly for the husband and the wife, it would seem unreasonable for the wife's solicitors to insist on a full abstract of title and investigation thereof. It must be assumed that the title was properly investigated at the time of the purchase by the husband and wife. It is suggested, therefore, that the husband's solicitors should submit to the wife's solicitors merely a copy of the last conveyance, together with a copy of any mortgage affecting the property and memoranda of any 'sales-off' or other documents affecting the legal title. In the case of registered land, sufficient particulars of the title or office copy entries of the registered title can be supplied to enable the wife's solicitors to draw a transfer.

Where the husband is not legally represented or has disappeared, then obviously the wife's solicitors should have complete conduct of the conveyancing and in these circumstances the wife's solicitors may have already asked the court to give an order to this effect (see Chapter 8). This should have the result that the title deeds will be released by any mortgagee to the wife's solicitors alone without the consent of the husband. In such circumstances the wife's solicitors will draw the conveyance or transfer by reference to the original title deeds in their hands.

Although the court order may specify a time-limit in which the conveyance or transfer must be completed, this is rarely adhered to. If an unreasonable time has elapsed and the husband refuses or fails to execute the conveyance or transfer, application can be made to the court (see Chapter 8).

For the reason that there can so often be delay in obtaining the husband's signature, it is recommended that only once the documentation has been agreed and executed is a 'completion date' arranged so that the wife's solicitors may (in the case of unregistered title) make a search against the husband at HM Land Charges Registry. In the case of registered title, if the wife is purchasing the husband's interest in the property, a search in usual form (Form 94A) at HM Land Registry is appropriate; otherwise a search should be made on Form 94C, although as the wife is a trustee of the legal estate with the husband, this search can be of little value, particularly as it confers no priority (Land Registration (Official Searches) Rules 1990 (SI No 1361), r 9).

As often as not, however, a mortgagee will be involved and priority can be obtained by the mortgagee's solicitors making a Form 94A search.

3 Form of conveyance or transfer

(a) Unregistered land

Where the husband and wife are beneficial joint tenants there are two methods by which the matrimonial home may be vested in the wife alone:

(i) the husband can release his interest in the legal estate to the wife (Law of Property Act 1925, s 36(2)); or

(ii) the husband and the wife can convey the legal estate to the wife alone (Law of Property Act 1925, s 72(4)).

Method (i) has been criticised (see Parker, *Modern Conveyancing Precedents*, Butterworths, 1964) but has stood the test of time (see *Kelly's Draftsman*—current 15th and earlier editions). It has been found in practice to be easy to explain to the lay client and easy for such a client to comprehend.

So far as a tenant in common is concerned however, he or she cannot release an undivided half share, as a tenant in common is solely seised of his or her respective interest. In this case, assuming that the trustees of the legal estate are tenants in common of the whole of the equity (as would usually be the case where husband and wife are concerned) a conveyance by the husband and the wife, as trustees of the legal estate, to the wife alone is the appropriate document. Whilst the conveyance will vest the legal estate in the wife, there should be an assignment by the husband to the wife of his equitable interest as well. So far as unregistered conveyancing is concerned, both transactions can take place in one document (see Precedent 27).

(b) Registered land

The rule of keeping the equities off the title is strictly enforced in registered conveyancing. Section 74 of the Land Registration Act 1925, provides that no person dealing with a registered estate or charge is to be affected with notice of a trust.

Thus, since neither the registry nor persons dealing with the registered estate can have notice of any trust a release by one joint tenant to another is inappropriate (in contrast to unregistered conveyancing) to transfer the registered estate, and a transfer from the husband and the wife to the wife alone is the appropriate document. Strictly the transfer should contain no reference to the husband's beneficial interest in the matrimonial home; this is a minor interest and will disappear with the alteration of the register (see *Key and Elphinstone's Precedents in Conveyancing*, 15th edn, vol 3, p 449, and *Hallett's Conveyancing Precedents*, Sweet and Maxwell, 1965, p 1286).

Such a transfer will be appropriate whether the property was held by the husband and wife as beneficial joint tenants or as tenants in common: in the latter case, as the transfer to the husband and wife will not have contained a declaration to the effect that the survivor of them could give a good receipt for capital monies, a restriction will have automatically been entered on the register to the effect that no disposition by a sole proprietor of the land (not being a trust corporation) under which capital money arises is to be registered except under an order of the registrar or of the court (Land Registration Act 1925, s 58(3) and Land Registration Rules 1925, r 213 as amended by Land Registration Rules 1989 (SI No 801)). When the property is transferred to the wife alone for her own absolute use, it is necessary, therefore, to appy to the registrar to remove this restriction (see Precedent 29). No fee is payable (Land Registration Fee Order 1992 (SI No 2089) Sched 4, Pt II).

As the transfer deals only with the legal estate, it can be argued that there should properly be a release off the register by the husband of his equitable interest in the matrimonial home to the wife. In practice such a release is rarely prepared, the parties being satisfied with the evidence of the court order and the transfer itself. Any purchaser from the wife is not concerned with this, as he is merely interested to check that the wife alone has power to transfer the property to him.

4 Covenants for title

Whilst the husband and wife as owners of the legal estate can make a conveyance or transfer as trustees to the wife alone as discussed in the previous section, there seems no good reason, when the husband conveys or releases his beneficial interest to the wife, why she should not receive the benefit of the 'beneficial owner' covenants (see Chapter 3).

As the beneficial owner covenants are only implied where there is valuable consideration, the covenants (in the absence of such consideration) should be expressly incorporated by reference thereto in the conveyance or transfer.

5 Where the property is subject to a mortgage

Although it may be agreed, or the court may order, that the matrimonial home be conveyed or transferred to the wife alone subject to the existing mortgage, the mortgagee may not be willing to release the husband therefrom. In such case there will be a conveyance or transfer to the wife alone subject to the existing mortgage with the husband taking an indemnity in respect thereof from the wife.

It will be recalled (see Chapter 3, p 35) that in the case of registered land, application under r 110 of the Land Registration Rules 1925 should be made to note this indemnity on the Register. The advantages of having the conveyance or transfer containing the indemnity executed in duplicate have already been noted (see Chapter 3, p 35).

If however, the mortgagee is prepared to rely on the wife's covenant, the husband can be released from liability by the mortgagee, with the wife alone remaining liable.

This may take place subsequent to the conveyance or transfer to the wife, so that a separate deed of release is required in favour of the husband (see Precedents 32 and 33). No stamp duty is payable on the deed (which should be prepared in duplicate so that the husband has evidence of his release). If it is required to register this release at HM Land Registry (and that depends on the practice by the mortgagee) the original (plus copy) should be sent (together with fee of £40) to HM Land Registry who would note on the Charges Register that the charge had been varied.

The wife will have already covenanted with the mortgagee in the original mortgage to repay the mortgage debt, and there is no need therefore for her to covenant further; surprisingly some mortgagees do, however, require this. Regard must therefore be had to the practice of each mortgagee in circumstances of this nature. Regard must also be had to *Williams & Glyn's Bank Ltd v Boland* [1981] AC 487 and the necessity for any consents to mortgage from those in occupation (see p 31 and Precedent 11).

It will be appreciated that if the conveyance or transfer is one of sale between the husband and wife as part of the matrimonial settlement, it can be advantageous for the purposes of stamp duty, inheritance tax and land registry fees to recite the amount of the mortgage debt and also to have a valuer's report. For stamp duty purposes, the consideration is increased to the extent that the husband's mortgage liability is released although this is not relevant if the transaction falls within s 83 Finance Act 1985 (see further Chapter 2).

6 Steps to be taken following the completion of the conveyance or transfer

(a) Stamp duty

A PD Form is required only if there has been a conveyance or transfer on sale (eg Precedent 17). If the consideration is less than £60,000 and the property already has registered title, the PD Form should be sent to HM Land Registry with the application for registration of the transfer (see The Stamp Duty (Exempt Instruments) Regulations 1985 (SI No 1688)).

Generally no stamp duty will be payable unless the conveyance is one on sale (or taking over of a mortgage liability) not resulting from a court order or agreement made in connection with the divorce (see Chapter 2).

(b) Court order and completion of abstract

In the case of registered land, a certified copy of the court order, or abstract thereof marked as examined against the original, should be delivered with the application to HM Land Registry for registration of the transfer.

In the case of unregistered land, a copy of the court order marked as examined against the original, or an abstract of the relevant portion of the order marked as examined against the original, should be placed with the title documents.

(c) First registration of title

Unless there is a conveyance of the *whole* (ie not just the husband's share or interest) of the property in the title, application for first registration of title in an area of compulsory registration is not necessary (Land Registration Act 1925, s 123). Therefore even though the wife may buy the husband's share (see Precedents 17 and 21), no application for first registration is required.

(d) HM Land Registry fees

Where the transfer is one on sale, the fees are based on the amount of the consideration in accordance with Scale A Land Registration Fees Order 1992 (SI No 2089).

Where the wife does not purchase the husband's interest, fees are based on the equivalent proportion of the value of the land which is the subject of the dealing after deducting therefrom an equivalent proportion of the amount secured on the land (by way of mortgage) and the fees can be ascertained from Scale A in Sched 1. Further, Sched 4, Pt I, Abatement 2(i), which will reduce the fee payable to one-fifth (subject to a minimum of £40), is available if claimed provided the transfer is made pursuant to an order of the court and is of the matrimonial home.

The value of the land may be evidenced by a statement from the solicitors lodging the application, which should specify the value of the property transferred. In practice this is either a letter or a statement of value on HM Land Registry Form A4.

(e) Insurance

Insurance of the property should be placed in the name of the wife alone, the husband's name being deleted from the policy. Otherwise, in the event of a claim the insurance company may insist on receiving the signature of both husband and wife before monies are paid out, and the husband's whereabouts at that time may not be known. Mortgagees should be reminded accordingly.

(f) Leasehold

The requirements of the lease as to registration of any assignment with the lessor should be observed.

*　*　*　*

PRECEDENTS

A—Notice of severance by husband to wife
severing joint tenancy

Precedent 12—Unregistered Land
To [*Wife's full name as in the conveyance and her address*]

I HEREBY GIVE YOU NOTICE severing our joint tenancy in equity of and in [*address of the matrimonial home preferably a description from the title deeds*] now held by yourself and myself as joint tenants both at law and in equity [and henceforth the property shall be held by us as tenants in common in equity in (equal) shares] AND I REQUEST you to acknowledge receipt of this Notice by signing and returning the Duplicate Notice enclosed herewith
Dated   [*Signature of Husband*]

Duplicate
　I acknowledge receipt of this Notice of Severance of which the above is a duplicate.
Dated   [*Signature of Wife*]

Precedent 13—Unregistered Land

Memorandum of Severance (endorsed on last conveyance)

By a Notice of Severance dated
addressed by the within named [*Husband*] to the within named [*Wife*] the beneficial joint tenancy herein created was severed.

Precedent 14—Registered Land

Application to enter a restriction
HM Land Registry

[Continue heading as Precedent 2]

Date   We [*husband*] of   and [*Wife*] of   apply to the Registrar to enter the following restriction against the title above referred to:

Restriction: No disposition by one proprietor of the land (being the survivor of joint proprietors and not being a trust corporation) under which capital money arises is to be registered except under an Order of the Registrar or of the Court.

SIGNED *etc* [*both parties*]

B—Conveyance by husband as joint tenant to wife as other joint tenant. No mortgage. By order of court

Precedent 15—Unregistered Land

THIS CONVEYANCE is made the   day of   19 BETWEEN (1) [*Husband*] of   ('the Husband') and (2) [*Wife*] of   ('the Wife')

WHEREAS:

(A) By a Conveyance ('the Conveyance') dated   and made between (1) [*previous vendor*] and (2) Husband and the Wife the Property herein described was conveyed to the Husband and the Wife in fee simple upon trust for themselves as beneficial joint tenants [subject as hereinafter mentioned but otherwise] free from incumbrances

[**Note**—*If the conveyance to the husband and wife was not to them 'as joint tenants' (ie upon the statutory trusts) the recital could be as follows*

(A) By a Conveyance (hereinafter called 'the Conveyance') dated   and made between (1) [*previous vendor*] and (2) the Husband and Wife the Property herein described was conveyed to the Husband and the Wife in fee simple upon trust to sell the same and to stand possessed of the net proceeds of sale and the net income until sale upon trust for themselves as joint tenants [subject as hereinafter mentioned but otherwise] free from incumbrances]

(B) By an Order of [Deputy] District Judge   in the   County Court dated   in proceedings between the Husband and the Wife bearing number   the Husband was ordered to convey all his estate and interest in the said property to the Wife
NOW pursuant to the Order THIS DEED WITNESSES:

1 The Husband as beneficial owner [*see p 30*] RELEASES AND CONVEYS [*see p 56*] to the Wife ALL THAT the estate and interest of

the Husband in ALL THAT *etc* [*parcels*] and in the net proceeds of sale and the net rents and profits thereof until sale TO HOLD the same to the Wife in fee simple to the intent that the Wife shall henceforth stand seised of the entirety of the Property free from any estate or interest of the Husband and free from the statutory trusts [SUBJECT to the covenants and conditions mentioned in the Conveyance so far as the same are still subsisting and capable of taking effect and affect the Property]

2 The Husband covenants with the Wife in the terms set out in Part I 2nd Schedule Law of Property Act 1925 [*see p 31*]

[3 *Covenant for indemnity if applicable—Precedent 1, clause 3*]

4 [*Stamp Duty Certificate—Precedent 1, clause 4*]

IN WITNESS whereof this deed has been duly executed the day and year before written

SIGNED as a Deed
by the Husband in the presence of:

SIGNED as a Deed
by the Wife in the presence of:

Precedent 16—Registered Land

[Same heading as Precedent 2]

Date   Pursuant to an Order of [Deputy] District Judge
          in the   County Court dated   in proceedings between the Transferor and the Transferee bearing number

1 We [*Husband*] of   formerly of   ('the Transferor') and [*Wife*] of   ('the Transferee') as trustees and by the direction of the Transferor directing as to all his interest therein as beneficial owner transfer to the Transferee the land comprised in the title above mentioned

2 The Transferor hereby covenants with the Transferee in the terms set out in Part 1 2nd Schedule Law of Property Act 1925 [*see p 32*]

3 [*Covenant for indemnity if applicable—see Precedent 2, clause 3*]

4 [*Stamp Duty Certificate—Precendent 1, clause 4*]

SIGNED as a Deed
by the Transferor in the presence of:

SIGNED as a Deed
by the Transferee in the presence of:

C—Conveyance by husband as joint tenant to wife as other joint tenant. Sale.
No mortgage

Precedent 17—Unregistered Land

THIS CONVEYANCE [*etc—see Precedent 15*]

WHEREAS:

(A) [*Seisin of the parties—Precedent 15 recital (A)*]

(B) The Husband has agreed with the Wife for the sale of all his estate and interest in the said property and in the proceeds of sale thereof to the Wife at a price of £

NOW pursuant to the agreement and in consideration of the sum of £   paid by the Wife to the Husband (the receipt of which the Husband acknowledges) THIS CONVEYANCE WITNESSES:

1 The Husband as beneficial owner RELEASES AND CONVEYS unto the Wife ALL THAT [*continue as Precedent 15, clause 1*]

[2 *Covenant for indemnity if appropriate—see Precedent 1, clause 3*]

3 [*Certificate of value—Precedent 9, clause 7*]

IN WITNESS *etc* [*see Precedent 15*]

Precedent 18—Registered Land

[*Same heading as Precedent 2*]

Date   In consideration of   pounds (£   ) paid to the Husband by the Wife (the receipt whereof the Husband hereby acknowledges)

1 We [*Husband*] of   formerly of   ('the Husband' and [*Wife*] of   ('the Wife') as trustees by the direction of the Husband directing as to all his interest therein as beneficial owner hereby transfer to the Wife the land comprised in the title above mentioned

[2 *Covenant for indemnity if appropriate—Precedent 2, clause 3*]

3 [*Certificate of value—Precedent 9, clause 7*]
SIGNED *etc* [*see Precedent 16*]

D—Conveyance by husband as joint tenant to wife as other joint tenant by order of court.
Mortgage. Husband released

Precedent 19—Unregistered Land

THIS CONVEYANCE is made the   day of 19   BETWEEN (1)
[*Husband*] of   ('the Husband') (2)   BUILD-
ING SOCIETY whose Chief Office is at   ('the Society')
and (3) [*Wife*] of   ('the Wife')

WHEREAS:

(A) [*Seisin of the parties—Precedent 15 recital (A)*]

(B) By a Mortgage ('the Mortgage') dated   and made
between (1) the Husband and the Wife and (2) the Society the Property
was charged to the Society to secure the sum of £

(C) The sum of £   is now owing to the Society on the security of the
Mortgage

(D) By an Order of [Deputy] District Judge   in the
               County Court dated   in proceedings
between the Husband and the Wife bearing number   the Husband
was ordered to convey all his estate and interest in the Property to the
Wife subject to the Mortgage

(E) The Society has agreed to release the Husband from his obligations
under the Mortgage

NOW pursuant to the Order THIS DEED WITNESSES:

1 The Husband as beneficial owner [*see p 30*] with the consent of the
Society RELEASES AND CONVEYS to the Wife ALL THAT the
estate and interest of the Husband in ALL THAT *etc* and in the net
proceeds of sale thereof and the net rents and profits thereof until sale
TO HOLD the same to the Wife in fee simple to the intent that the Wife
shall henceforth stand seised of the entirety of the Property free from
any estate or interest of the Husband and free from the statutory trusts
SUBJECT to the Mortgage and all principal money and interest thereby
secured [and SUBJECT ALSO (*continue as Precedent 15, clause 1*)]

2 THE Society releases and discharges the Husband from his obligations under the Mortgage

3 THE Husband covenants with the Wife in the terms set out in Part I
2nd Schedule Law of Property Act 1925 [*see p 31*]

[4 *Covenant for indemnity if applicable—See Precedent 1, clause 3*]

5 [*Stamp Duty Certificate—Precedent 1, clause 4*]
  IN WITNESS *etc* [*see Precedent 5*]

Precedent 20—Registered Land

[*Same heading as Precedent 2*]

Date   Pursuant to an Order of [Deputy] District Judge
            in the   County Court dated   in
proceedings between the Transferor and the Transferee bearing number

1 We [*Husband*] of   formerly of   ('the
Transferor') and [*Wife*] of   ('the Transferee') as trustees by
direction of the Transferor directing as to all his interest therein as
beneficial owner transfer to the Transferee the land comprised in the
title above mentioned SUBJECT to the Charge ('the Registered
Charge') dated   and registered on   under
which there is now owing the sum of £

2 The   Building Society ('the Society') of
being the registered proprietor of the Registered Charge releases and
discharges the Transferor from all obligations under the Registered
Charge

3 The Transferor covenants with the Transferee in the terms set out in
Part I 2nd Schedule Law of Property Act 1925

[4 *Covenant for indemnity if applicable — Precedent 2, clause 3*]

5 [*Stamp Duty Certificate — Precedent 1, clause 4*]

SIGNED as a Deed
by the Transferor in the presence of:

SIGNED as a Deed
by the Transferee in the presence of:

THE COMMON SEAL of the
Society was hereunto affixed
in the presence of:

[OR for companies authorised not to use a seal see Precedent 5]

E—Conveyance by husband as joint tenant to wife as other joint tenant. Sale. Mortgage. Husband released

Precedent 21 — Unregistered Land

THIS CONVEYANCE *etc* [*parties as Precedent 19*]

WHEREAS:

(A) [*Seisin of the parties — Precedent 15, recital (A)*]

(B) [*Recital of the mortgage — Precedent 19, recital (B)*]

(C) [*Recital of the mortgage debt — Precedent 19, recital (C)*]

(D) The Husband has agreed with the Wife for the sale to her subject to the Mortgage of all his estate and interest in the Property and in the proceeds of sale thereof

(E) [*Recital as to release by mortgagee—Precedent 19, recital (E)*]

NOW pursuant to the agreement and in consideration of the sum of £   paid by the Wife to the Husband (the receipt of which the Husband acknowledges) THIS CONVEYANCE WITNESSES:

1 THE Husband as beneficial owner with the consent of the Society RELEASES AND CONVEYS unto the Wife ALL THAT *etc* [*continue as Precedent 19, clause 1*]

2 [*Release of the husband—Precedent 19, clause 2*]

3 [*Covenant for indemnity if appropriate—Precedent 1, clause 3*]

4 [*Certificate of value—Precedent 9, clause 7*]

    IN WITNESS *etc* [*see Precedent 5*]

Precedent 22—Registered Land

[*Same heading as Precedent 2*]

Date   In consideration of   pounds (£   ) paid by the Transferee to the Transferor (the receipt whereof the Transferor hereby acknowledges) We [*Husband*] [*continue as Precedent 20, clause 1*]

2 [*Release of the husband—Precedent 20, clause 2*]

3 [*Covenant for indemnity if appropriate—Precedent 2, clause 3*]

4 [*Certificate of value—Precedent 9, clause 7*]

SIGNED *etc* [*see Precedent 20*]

F—Assignment of leasehold property by husband as joint tenant to wife as other joint tenant. By agreement subject to mortgage. Husband released

Precedent 23—Unregistered Land
THIS ASSIGNMENT is made the   day of 19   BETWEEN (1) [*Husband*] of   ('the Husband') (2)   Building Society whose Chief Office is at   ('the Society') and (3) [*Wife*] of   ('the Wife')

WHEREAS:

(A) By a Lease ('the Lease') dated   and made between (1) X and (2) Y the property hereinafter described was demised by X to Y for the term of [99] years subject to the rent thereby reserved and to the covenants and conditions therein contained

(B) The premises demised by the Lease are now vested in the Husband and the Wife as beneficial joint tenants for the residue of the term granted by the Lease subject as aforesaid

(C) By a Mortgage ('the Mortgage') dated   and made between (1) the Husband and the Wife and (2) the Society the Property was charged to the Society to secure the sum of £

(D) The sum of £   is now owing to the Society on the security of the Mortgage

(E) The Husband has agreed to transfer his interest in the Property to the Wife

(F) The Society has agreed to release the Husband from his obligations under the Mortgage

NOW pursuant to the agreement THIS DEED WITNESSES:

1 The Husband as beneficial owner with the consent of the Society RELEASES AND ASSIGNS to the Wife ALL THAT the estate and interest of the Husband in ALL THAT *etc* being the property comprised in and demised by the Lease and the net proceeds of sale thereof and the net rents and profits until sale TO HOLD the same to the Wife for all the residue now unexpired by the term of years granted by the Lease TO THE INTENT that the Wife shall henceforth stand seised of the entirety of the said property free from any estate or interest of the Husband therein and free also from the statutory trusts SUBJECT to the Mortgage and all principal money and interest thereby received and SUBJECT henceforth to the payment of rent reserved by and to the covenants and conditions contained or referred to in the Lease and on the part of the Lessee to be observed and performed

2 The Society releases and discharges the Husband from his obligations under the Mortgage

3 The Husband covenants with the Wife in the terms set out in Part I and Part II 2nd Schedule Law of Property Act 1925 and the Wife covenants with the Husband in the terms set out in Part IX 2nd Schedule Law of Property Act 1925

4 It is certified that this instrument falls within category H in the Schedule to The Stamp Duty (Exempt Instruments) Regulations 1987

IN WITNESS *etc* [*see Precedent 5*]

Precedent 24—Registered Land
[*Same heading as Precedent 2*]

Date

1 We [*Husband*] of   formerly of   ('the Transferor')
and [*Wife*] of   ('the Transferee') as trustees by direction of
the Transferor directing as to all his interest therein as beneficial owner
hereby transfer to the Transferee the land comprised in the above title
for the residue of the term granted by the registered Lease SUBJECT to
the Charge ('the Registered Charge') dated   and registered
on   under which there is now owing the sum of £

2 The   Building Society of   being the registered
proprietor of the Registered Charge releases and discharges the Transferor from all obligations under the Registered Charge

3 The Transferor covenants with the Transferee in the terms set out in
Part I and Part II 2nd Schedule Law of Property Act 1925 and the
Transferee covenants with the Transferor in the terms set out in Part IX
2nd Schedule Law of Property Act 1925

4 [*Stamp Duty Certificate—see Precedent 23*]

SIGNED *etc* [*see Precedent 6*]

G—Conveyance by husband as joint tenant to wife as other joint tenant by order of court. Mortgage. Husband not released but wife indemnifying him. Mortgagee not a party (see p 59)

Precedent 25—Unregistered Land

THIS CONVEYANCE is made the   day of   19
BETWEEN (1) [*Husband*] of   ('the Husband') and (2)
[*Wife*] of   ('the Wife')

WHEREAS:

(A) [*Seisin of the parties—Precedent 15, recital (A)*]

(B) [*Recital of the mortgage–Precedent 19, recital (B)*]

(C) [*Recital of court order—Precedent 19, recital (D)*]

NOW pursuant to the Order this Deed WITNESSES:

1 THE Husband as beneficial owner [*see p 30*] RELEASES AND
CONVEYS to the Wife [*continue as Precedent 19, clause 1*]

2 THE Husband covenants with the Wife in the terms set out in Part I
2nd Schedule Law of Property Act 1925 [*see p 31*]

3 THE Wife covenants with the Husband that with effect from [*date*] she
will pay and discharge all principal monies interest costs and other

monies secured by or henceforth to become payable under the Mortgage and will comply with the covenants therein and will at all times indemnify and keep indemnified the Husband and his estate and effects against all proceedings costs claims and demands in respect thereof

[4 *Covenant for indemnity if appropriate — Precedent 1, clause 3*]

5 [*Stamp Duty Certificate — Precedent 1, clause 4*]

IN WITNESS *etc* [*see Precedent 15*]

Precedent 26 — Registered Land

[*Same heading as Precedent 2*]

Date   In pursuance of an Order [*continue as Precedent 20*]

1 [*Transfer — Precedent 20, clause 1*]

2 [*Covenant by husband — Precedent 20, clause 3*]

3 With effect from [*date*] the Transferee covenants with the Transferor that she will pay and discharge all principal monies interest costs and other monies secured or henceforth to become payable under the Registered Charge and will comply with the covenants therein and will at all times indemnify and keep indemnified the Transferor and his estate and effects against all proceedings costs claims and demands in respect thereof AND the Transferor and Transferee hereby make application to the Registrar (under Rule 110 Land Registration Rules 1925) to note this covenant on the Register [*see p 35*]

[4 *Covenant for indemnity if appropriate — Precedent 2, clause 3*]

5 [*Stamp Duty Certificate — Precedent 1, clause 4*]

SIGNED *etc* [*see Precedent 16*]

H — Conveyance by husband to wife. Sale of his share in matrimonial home held by them as tenants in common in equal shares. No mortgage

[*If the tenants in common do not hold in equal shares, alteration should be made accordingly, and if the shares are not known then the husband should assign 'all that his share'*]

Precedent 27 — Unregistered Land

THIS CONVEYANCE is made the   day of   19
BETWEEN (1) [*Husband*] of   ('the Husband') (2) the
Husband and [*Wife*] of   (the last named being called 'the
Wife') and (3) the Wife

WHEREAS:

(A) By a Conveyance ('the Conveyance') dated   and made between (1)   and (2) the Husband and the Wife the Property herein described was conveyed to the Husband and the Wife and vested in them as tenants in common in [equal] shares [subject as therein mentioned but otherwise] free from incumbrances

(B) The Husband has agreed with the Wife for the sale to her of all his share and interest in the Property in equity and in the proceeds of sale thereof for the sum £   and the Wife has requested that the Property should be vested in the Wife alone

NOW THIS DEED made in consideration of £   paid by the Wife to the Husband (the receipt of which the Husband acknowledges) WITNESSES:

1 THE Husband as beneficial owner in respect of his one [half] share in the proceeds of sale of the Property ASSIGNS and the Husband and the Wife as trustees in respect of the legal estate therein CONVEY to the Wife ALL *etc* [*parcels*] TO HOLD the same to the Wife in fee simple discharged from the statutory trusts and from all the estate right or interest of the Husband therein

[2 *Covenant for indemnity if appropriate—Precedent 1, clause 3*]

3 [*Certificate of value—Precedent 9, clause 7*]

   IN WITNESS *etc* [*see Precedent 15*]

Precedent 28—Unregistered Land (the joint tenancy having been severed)

THIS CONVEYANCE [*continue as Precedent 27*]

WHEREAS:

(A) [*Recital of conveyance to husband and wife—Precedent 15, recital (A)*]

(B) By notice in writing dated   and given by the Husband to the Wife the Husband terminated the beneficial joint tenancy created between the Husband and the Wife by the Conveyance

(C) [*Recital of agreement for sale—Precedent 27, recital (B)*]

NOW THIS DEED [*continue as Precedent 27*]

1 [*Assignment and conveyance—Precedent 27, clause 1*]

[2 *Covenant for indemnity if appropriate—Precedent 1, clause 3*]

3 [*Certificate of value—Precedent 9, clause 7*]

   [IN WITNESS *etc* [*see Precedent 15*]

D

Precedent 29—Registered Land

[*Same heading as Precedent 2*]

Date   In consideration of   pounds (£   )
paid by the Transferee to the Transferor (the receipt of which the
Transferor acknowledges)

1 We [*Husband*] of
formerly of
('the Transferor') and [*Wife*] of
('the Transferee') as trustees by direction of the Transferor directing as
to all his interest therein as beneficial owner transfer to the Transferee
the land comprised in the title above mentioned

2 The Transferor and the Transferee hereby apply to the Registrar to
withdraw the restriction registered on the   day of   against
the title above referred to

[3 *Covenant for indemnity if appropriate—Precedent 2, clause 3*]

4 [*Certificate of value—Precedent 9, clause 7*]

SIGNED *etc* [*see Precedent 16*]

I—Conveyance by husband to wife by order of court
of his share in matrimonial home
held by them as tenants in common. No mortgage

Precedent 30—Unregistered Land

THIS CONVEYANCE [*continue as Precedent 27*]

WHEREAS:

(A) [*Seisin of the parties—Precedent 27, recital (A) or Precedent 15,
recital (A) and Precedent 28, recital (B)*]

(B) By an Order of [Deputy] District Judge   in the
                County Court dated   in proceedings
between the Husband and the Wife bearing number   the
Husband was ordered to assign and convey all his share and interest in
the Property to the Wife

NOW pursuant to the Order THIS DEED WITNESSES:

1 [*Assignment and conveyance—Precedent 27, clause 1*]

[2 *Covenant for indemnity if appropriate—Precedent 1, clause 3*]

3 [*Stamp Duty Certificate—Precedent 1, clause 4*]

IN WITNESS *etc* [*see Precedent 15*]

Precedent 31—Registered Land

[*Same heading as Precedent 2*]

Date   Pursuant to an Order of [Deputy] District Judge
            in the   County Court dated   in
proceedings between the Transferor and the Transferee bearing number

1 [*Precedent 29, clause 1*]

2 [*Precedent 29, clause 2*]

3 [*Covenant for indemnity if appropriate—Precedent 2, clause 3*]

4 [*Stamp Duty Certificate—Precedent 1, clause 4*]

SIGNED *etc* [*see Precedent 16*]

J—Release of husband from mortgage by mortgagee at date subsequent to conveyance to wife subject to the mortgage (see page 58)

Precedent 32—Unregistered Land
Date
            Building Society hereby releases and discharges
            [*Husband*] from all obligations under the Legal Charge
dated   over the property known as [1 Blackacre Drive, Blackacre]

THE COMMON SEAL OF The
BUILDING SOCIETY was hereunto
affixed in the presence of:

Precedent 33—Registered Land

[HM LAND REGISTRY]

County and District
or London Borough

Title Number

Property

Date
            Building Society hereby releases and discharges
            [*Husband*] from all obligations under the Legal Charge
dated   and registered on

[*Attestation as Precedent 32*]

Chapter 5

Conveyance of Husband's Interest to New Husband

This chapter deals principally with the situation where the husband and the wife hold the matrimonial home in their joint names (whether as beneficial joint tenants or as tenants in common) and, as a result of property adjustments, the husband's interest in the home is conveyed or transferred to the wife's new husband or friend. The expression 'new husband' used in this chapter will include another person, whether the wife is married to him or not.

With the court having ordered the husband's interest to be conveyed or transferred to the wife, or agreement to that effect having been reached, it may be that the wife requests or desires that the house be conveyed or transferred to herself and her new husband. Alternatively, the new husband may agree to purchase the husband's interest therein. In either event, particular regard will have to be had to the capital gains tax, inheritance tax and stamp duty implications of such a transaction, and whilst these are dealt with more fully in Chapter 2, the following points are mentioned as an *aide-mémoire*:

> (i) If the new husband purchases the husband's interest in the house, is this for full value and on the basis of an arm's length transaction? If not, there could be a potential liability for inheritance tax.
>
> (ii) If the wife becomes entitled to the whole house and requests that the matrimonial home be conveyed or transferred to herself and her 'new husband' (to whom she is not married), is the wife making a gift for inheritance tax purposes to the 'new husband'?
>
> (iii) The Inland Revenue capital gains tax concession men-

74

tioned in Chapter 2 may not be available (on a strict interpretation of its wording) to the *former* husband if he conveys or transfers his interest in his former principal private residence to someone other than his spouse or ex-spouse.

(iv) A conveyance to someone other than a party to the marriage will not attract the stamp duty relief of s 83 of the Finance Act 1985, (see p 22) but if it is a voluntary disposition, exemption L of The Stamp Duty (Exempt Instruments) Regulations 1987 (SI No 516) (Chapter 2) will apply. In view of the stamp duty implications, the wife should consider taking the conveyance herself and subsequently conveying to herself and the new husband.

The potential threat of the conveyance to the wife and new husband being put aside if the sale to the new husband could be considered to be at an undervalue must be borne in mind (see p 5 and Insolvency Act 1986, s 339).

1 Procedure

(a) Is the wife entitled to have the house conveyed/transferred to herself and new husband?

If the court has ordered the husband (or the husband has agreed) to convey or transfer his interest in the former matrimonial home to the wife, there is no reason why he should agree, at the request of the wife, to convey or transfer it to herself and her new husband. If he does not so agree, then the Precedents in Chapters 3 and 4 are appropriate, and it is up to the wife to make a further conveyance or deed of gift once the property is vested in herself alone. Suitable precedents can be found in *Kelly's Draftsman*, 15th edn, Butterworths, 1986, or in the *Encyclopedia of Forms and Precedents*, 5th edn, Butterworths, 1989, Vol 17.

If the wife and new husband are purchasing the husband's share or interest in the property for full value, then usual sale and purchase considerations apply. If, however, it is agreed that the wife should purchase the husband's share and interest, and in reality the purchase monies are being provided by the new husband, then if the husband refuses to convey his interest in the house to the wife and the new husband, it is suggested that the wife takes the conveyance/transfer in her sole name as nominee and makes a subsequent conveyance to herself and the new husband.

This latter conveyance (for which there is a suitable precedent which can be adapted from *Kelly's Draftsman*, 15th edn, p 655) will require stamp duty of 50p and the production of the original conveyance to the wife.

(b) Contract

Where the arrangement is agreed between the parties, the practitioner must consider whether or not it is desirable to have a binding contract. If the husband is purchasing a house for himself with the proceeds of sale of his interest in the matrimonial home, then, as he will have to commit himself to a contract in respect of his purchase, it is suggested that there should be a contract relating to the sale of his interest in the matrimonial home so that he is fully safeguarded. This should ensure an adherence to a timetable which otherwise might be lacking in the case of an agreement between the parties not supported by a binding contract.

(c) Conduct of the conveyancing

It is appropriate for the husband's solicitors to obtain the title deeds so that they may act as vendor's solicitors. It is envisaged that the wife and the new husband will have a solicitor who acts for both of them.

Whilst the new husband is entitled to have the title investigated fully (at his own cost), in a case where the house is already in the joint names of the husband and wife, it is thought that, in practice, the new husband will rely upon the title at the time of the conveyance to the husband and the wife having been properly investigated. In the case of unregistered title the husband's solicitors will, therefore, submit a copy of the last conveyance, mortgage (if any), any sales-off or other transactions, together with copies of any covenants referred to in the last conveyance, to the new husband's solicitors who will themselves submit a draft conveyance. In the case of registered title, office copy entries of the registered title can be supplied to enable the wife's and new husband's solicitors to draw the relevant transfer.

Unless there is a contract governing the transaction, it is suggested that when the conveyance or transfer has been executed by all parties a completion date should be arranged so that the necessary searches can be made by reference to that date and the matter completed. In the case of unregistered title, a search at HM Land Charges Registry against both the husband and the wife should be made, whilst a Form 94A Search is appropriate in the case of registered land (except in the case of Precedent 41 when a Form 94C Search is appropriate. It will be recalled that this does not confer priority (see Chapter 3, p 30)).

2 Covenants for title

The husband, even in the absence of valuable consideration, should assign his share or interest in the matrimonial home as 'beneficial owner' for the reasons set out in Chapter 3. The effect of the 'beneficial owner' covenants in respect of leasehold property is also mentioned in Chapter 3.

Where the wife takes the conveyance and requires it to be conveyed to herself and the new husband, she should convey as 'trustee' (thus implying that she herself has not encumbered the property) as she has never had the legal title vested in her absolutely.

3 Form of the conveyance or transfer

(a) Unregistered land

Recitals to a conveyance can be very useful, not only to describe briefly the reason for the deed but also to recite additional information which, owing to the provisions of s 45(6) of the Law of Property Act 1925 (the section providing that a recital 20 years' old shall be sufficient evidence of the truth of the fact recited unless proved to the contrary), might not be readily available later (for instance, because a copy marriage certificate is mislaid or was not abstracted). With this in mind, it may be prudent if the wife has remarried to recite details of that marriage (as in Precedent 34).

If the joint tenancy between the husband and wife has been severed, it will have been possible for the husband to mortgage his own share or settle it upon certain trusts. Although the wife, as the other trustee of the conveyance, should have received notice of any incumbrance (see *Dearle v Hall* (1828) 3 Russ 1), it is as well if the conveyance to the wife and new husband contains a recital that the property is free from incumbrances (assuming this to be so) to stop any requisitions on a later sale and also to direct the parties' attention to any incumbrances if there have been such.

Although all that is required, where the new husband is acquiring the husband's interest, is an assignment of the husband's equitable interest, this is plainly impracticable as neither the new husband nor the wife will wish the husband to continue to have any interest at all in the property. The precedents which follow, therefore, contain not only an assignment of the husband's equitable interest in the property but also a conveyance of the legal estate to new trustees.

Where the wife and new husband are to hold as beneficial joint tenants it is not strictly necessary to incorporate an express power of sale and purport to extend the powers of the trustees of the conveyance in the conveyance since the Law of Property Act 1925 (ss 35 and 36) already implies that they will hold upon the 'statutory trusts'. However, if it is thought that the joint tenancy might be severed (and there might be good matrimonial or tax planning reasons for this) it is preferable to include the enlargement of powers as in Precedent 34 for otherwise the trustees of the conveyance may not have power to mortgage or charge the property (see Perpetuities and Accumulations Act 1964, s 8).

(b) Registered land

The approved Land Registry transfer (Form 19 JP) can be adapted to meet the situations covered in this chapter. So far as the wife and new husband are concerned, in contrast to unregistered title it is not necessary to declare that the registered proprietors have the powers of an absolute owner in dealing with the registered land. Sections 18 and 21 of the Land Registration Act 1925 provide that a registered proprietor can exercise all powers of disposition unless there be some entry on the register to the contrary.

It will be recalled (see Chapter 4, p 53) that the registrar is not affected with notice of any trust and that references to trusts are excluded from the register so far as possible (Land Registration Act 1925, s 74). Unless the registrar is instructed to the contrary, a transfer to the wife and new husband will result in the registration of a restriction to the effect that no disposition by a sole proprietor of the land (not being a trust corporation) under which capital money arises is to be registered except under an order of the Registrar or of the Court (ie the survivor of the wife and new husband cannot give a good receipt for capital monies) (Land Registration Act 1925, s 58(3) and Land Registration Rules 1925 (SR & O 1925 No 1093, r 213 as amended by Land Registration Rules 1989, SI No 801)). If in effect, therefore, the wife and new husband wish to hold the property as beneficial joint tenants, they must make the declaration contained in Precedent 35.

However it is suggested (see Newsletter Issue 1/93, Sweet and Maxwell) that the cases of *Huntingdon v Hobbs* [1992] EGCS 38 and *Springette v Defoe* [1992] Fam Law 459 show that as between the co-owners the Court will not regard the simple statement that the survivor can give a good receipt in the printed Form 19 (JP) as decisive of the existence of a beneficial joint tenancy; thus the additional wording to the declaration (see Precedent 35, clause 2).

If the wife and new husband wish to hold as tenants in common, then it must be remembered that the register will not show their respective shares and they should make a separate declaration (which will be off the register) as to these, and this will be evidence at a later date should their shares be in dispute (for instance with the trustee in bankruptcy of either party). If the transfer refers to the shares of the tenants in common, it is thought that this is unobjectionable to the registrar, although no note of the shares will appear on the register. The registrar does have a discretion to allow inspection of a filed transfer (Land Registration Rules 1925, r 290(1)); but it is obviously better either to have a duplicate of the transfer or a separate declaration of trust so that exercise of the discretion does not have to be requested. This would in any event take time.

4 Where the property is subject to a mortgage

If the property is subject to a mortgage, then if the new husband's financial status is acceptable to the mortgagee it will doubtless be prepared to release the husband's covenant in return for receiving a similar covenant from the new husband. The exact requirements of the mortgagee to be contained in the conveyance or transfer should be ascertained.

The necessity of obtaining consent to transfer subject to a mortgage from any other occupier of the matrimonial home aged 18 years or over should not be overlooked (*Williams & Glyn's Bank Ltd v Boland* [1981] AC 487). (See Precedent 11.)

If the new husband's financial status is not acceptable to the mortgagee, so that the mortgagee is only prepared to agree to a conveyance of the property to the wife and new husband if the husband remains liable under the original mortgage, then it would seem reasonable for the husband to comply only with the terms of the court order or matrimonial agreement (to which of course the new husband is not a party) and not to convey/transfer to the wife and the new husband. If the husband is prepared to remain liable under the mortgage he should remain a trustee of the legal estate (which could stand in the names of the husband, the wife and new husband) so that he will know the state of the mortgage account and so that a further advance or a second charge cannot be created without his consent.

In a case where the husband owns the house alone, subject to mortgage, and the wife and new husband decide to buy him out, the most usual procedure would be for the conveyance to the wife and new husband to take place contemporaneously with the redemption of the existing mortgage and the taking of the new mortgage.

5 Steps to be taken following the completion of the conveyance or transfer

(a) Stamp duty

Where there has been a conveyance or transfer on sale a PD Form will be required; if the consideration is less than £60,000 and the property already has registered title, the PD Form should be sent to HM Land Registry with the application for registration of the transfer (the Stamp Duty (Exempt Instruments) Regulations 1985 (SI No 1688)).

None of the conveyances which are the subject of this chapter fall within the provisions of s 83 of the Finance Act 1985 for they are not conveyances from one party to the marriage to the other. For those conveyances on sale where the consideration (including any mortgage debt assumed) is less than £60,000, a certificate of value will be required (see Chapter 2). Where this figure is exceeded *ad valorem* stamp duty will be payable.

Precedents 40 to 43 are a hybrid between the relief under s 83 and heading L (Voluntary Disposition) of The Stamp Duty (Exempt Instruments) Regulations 1987 (SI No 516) and it is suggested that the document should be submitted for adjudication. No stamp duty should be payable because of these reliefs but the Regulations do not provide for a hybrid certificate.

In contrast, Precedents 44 and 45 should contain two certificates (depending on the consideration) as they include a conveyance by court order to the wife and a sale. No stamp duty will be payable if the consideration for the latter is less than £60,000.

(b) Completion of the abstract

In those cases where it is recited that the wife has married the new husband, a marked copy of the marriage certificate or marked abstract thereof should be placed with the title documents (Precedents 34 and 38). Generally speaking, any recital must be supported by proof of a marked or examined copy of the document giving rise to the recital. Thus, a marked copy of the court order or an abstract thereof marked as examined against the original should be lodged either within the deeds or at HM Land Registry in the circumstances of Precedents 40 to 43.

Where in registered land a new covenant is given by the new husband to the mortgagee, the mortgagee may require a certified copy of the transfer containing the covenant to be lodged with the deeds so that it has a proper record of the liability of the new husband, the transfer incorporating the covenant itself being at the Land Registry.

(c) First registration of title

Generally, an application for first registration of title, even when the land is in a compulsory area, will not be required unless the conveyance has been one of sale of the *whole* of the property (Land Registration Act 1925, s 123). (See also Ruoff and Roper, *Registered Conveyancing*, Looseleaf edn, 1991, §11–07.)

(d) HM Land Registry fees

The purchase by the new husband of the husband's share in the former matrimonial home is a dealing for value within the Land Registration Fees Order 1992 (SI No 2089) and fees under Article 2, Scale A, of the Fee Order will be payable on the amount or value of the consideration. However, where the transfer is pursuant to a court order or does not otherwise involve consideration.

Abatement 2 of Sched 4, Pt I will be applicable thus reducing the fee to one-fifth with a minimum of £40, (see Chapter 3, p 38). The value of the land should be specified by the solicitor lodging the application to the Land Registry by letter or on Form A4.

(e) Registered land—adjudication

If adjudication for stamp duty purposes appears necessary (see (a) above) one must bear in mind that the time taken would usually exceed the priority period provided by the new husband's Land Registry search. The transfer should, therefore, first be sent (with a certified copy) to HM Land Registry with a written request for its immediate return for adjudication purposes and an undertaking that as soon as it has been adjudicated it will be relodged. In these circumstances, an applicant will not lose his priority (Land Registration Rules 1925, r 95). The Land Registry will return the original transfer so that it can be lodged with the adjudication section of the Stamp Office within the thirty-day lodging period.

(f) Insurance

The appropriate changes should be made to delete the husband's name from the policy and add that of the new husband.

*   *   *   *

PRECEDENTS

A—Conveyance on sale by one joint tenant (husband) to stranger (new husband). Remaining joint tenant (wife) and stranger becoming joint tenants. No mortgage

Precedent 34—Unregistered Land

THIS CONVEYANCE is made the   day of   19

BETWEEN (1) [*Husband*] of   ('the Husband') (2) [*Wife*]
of   ('the Wife') and (3) [*New Husband*] of
('*NH*')

WHEREAS:

(A) By a Conveyance ('the Conveyance') dated   and
made between (1)   and (2) the Husband and the Wife (the
Wife being then in the Conveyance called [*Mrs H*]) the Property herein
described was conveyed to the Husband and the Wife in fee simple
UPON TRUST for themselves as beneficial joint tenants [subject as
hereinafter mentioned but otherwise] free from incumbrances

(B) The marriage between the Husband and the Wife having been
dissolved the Wife became the Wife of *NH* on   at

(C) The Husband has agreed with *NH* for the sale to him of all his estate
and interest in the Property and in the proceeds of sale thereof for the
sum of £   and it has been agreed between the Wife and *NH* that they
should hold the Property as beneficial joint tenants

NOW THIS DEED made in consideration of the sum of £   paid by
NH to the Husband (the receipt of which the Husband acknowledges)
WITNESSES:

1 The Husband and Wife as trustees by direction of the Husband
directing as to all his share and interest therein as beneficial owner
convey to the Wife and *NH* ALL THAT *etc* TO HOLD the same to the
Wife and *NH* as joint tenants in fee simple [SUBJECT (*continue as
Precedent 1, clause 1*)]

2 [*Covenant for indemnity if applicable*
   The Wife and *NH* covenant with the Husband to observe and perform
the said covenants and conditions and to keep the Husband and his
personal representatives effectually indemnified against all losses resulting from their non-observance or breach so far as aforesaid]

3 The Wife and NH declare that:
   (a) They hold the Property and its net proceeds of sale and the net
       income until sale on trust for themselves as beneficial joint
       tenants
   (b) The trustees of this deed shall have all the powers of an
       absolute owner to deal with the Property

4 [*Certificate of value—Precedent 9, clause 7*]

IN WITNESS whereof this deed has been duly executed the day and
year before written

SIGNED as a Deed
by the Husband in the presence of:

SIGNED as a Deed
by the Wife in the presence of:

SIGNED as a Deed
by *NH* in the presence of:

Precedent 35—Registered Land

[Same heading as Precedent 2]

Date

1 In consideration of   pounds (£   ) paid by [*NH*] to the
Transferor (the receipt of which the Transferor hereby acknowledges)
[*Husband*] of   ('the Transferor') and [*Wife*] of
     ('the Wife') as trustees by direction of the Transferor
directing as to all his interest therein as beneficial owner transfer to the
Wife and [*NH*] of   ('*NH*') the land comprised in the title
above mentioned

2 *NH* and the Wife declare that the survivor of them can give a good
receipt for capital monies and that they are beneficial joint tenants

3 [*Covenant for indemnity if applicable*:
NH and the Wife covenant with the Transferor to observe and perform
the covenants and conditions referred to in the Charges Register so far
as still subsisting and relate to the Property and to keep the Transferor
and his personal representatives effectually indemnified against all losses
resulting from their non-observance or breach so far as aforesaid]

4 [*Certificate of value—Precedent 9, clause 7*]

SIGNED *etc* [*see Precedent 34. All three parties will need to execute the
transfer*]

**B—Conveyance on sale by husband of share in matrimonial
home (held by self and wife as tenants in common in equal
shares) to new husband. Wife and new husband holding as
tenants in common in equal shares. No mortgage**

Precedent 36—Unregistered Land

THIS CONVEYANCE is made the   day of   19
BETWEEN (1) [*Husband*] of   ('the Husband') (2) the
Husband and [*Wife*] ('the Wife') of   (the Husband and the
Wife being together called 'the Trustees') (3) [*NH*] of
('*NH*') and (4) *NH* and the Wife ('the New Trustees')

WHEREAS:

(A) [*Seisin of the Husband and Wife—Precedent 27, recital (A)*]

(B) The Trustees are the persons now entitled to the whole beneficial interest in the said Property free from incumbrances and subsidiary trusts

(C) The Husband has agreed with *NH* for the sale to him of all his share in the proceeds of sale of the said Property at the price of £   and the Trustees have agreed to join in this Deed in manner hereinafter appearing

NOW THIS DEED made in consideration of £   paid by *NH* to the Husband (the receipt of which the Husband acknowledges) WITNESSES:

1 THE Husband as beneficial owner assigns to *NH* ALL THAT the [one half] share of the Husband in equity in ALL *etc* [*parcels*] TO HOLD the same to *NH* absolutely

2 THE Trustees as trustees hereby convey the Property to the New Trustees TO HOLD the same to the New Trustees as joint tenants in fee simple free from the statutory trusts.

3 The Wife and *NH* declare that:
    (a) They hold the Property and its net proceeds of sale and the net income until sale on trust for themselves as tenants in common in equal shares
    (b) The trustees of this deed shall have all the powers of an absolute owner to deal with the Property

[4 *Covenant for indemnity if applicable—Precedent 34, clause 2 substituting 'The New Trustees' for 'The Wife and NH'*]

5 [*Certificate of value—Precedent 9, clause 7*]

   IN WITNESS *etc* [*see Precedent 34*]

Precedent 37—Registered Land

[Same heading as Precedent 2]

Date .

1 In consideration of   pounds (£   ) paid by [*NH*] of
          ('*NH*') to [*Husband*] of   ('the Husband')
(the receipt of which the Husband hereby acknowledges) the Husband and [*Wife*] of   ('the Wife') as trustees and by direction of the Husband directing as to [one equal half] share in the proceeds of sale as beneficial owner transfer to the Wife and *NH* the land comprised in the title above mentioned

[2 *Covenant for indemnity if applicable—see Precedent 35, clause 3*]

3 [*Certificate of value—Precedent 9, clause 7*]

SIGNED [*see Precedent 34*]

C—Conveyance on sale by husband of share in matrimonial home. Husband and wife joint tenants. Wife and new husband taking as tenants in common. Mortgage. Wife and new husband responsible. Husband released

Precedent 38—Unregistered Land

THIS CONVEYANCE is made the   day of   19
BETWEEN (1) [*Husband*] of   ('the Husband') (2) [*Wife*]
of   ('the Wife') (3)   BUILDING SOCIETY
whose chief office is at   ('the Society') and (4) [*New
Husband*] of   ('*NH*')

WHEREAS:

(A) By a Conveyance ('the Conveyance') dated   and
made between (1)   and (2) the Husband and the Wife (the
Wife being then and in the Conveyance called [*Mrs H*]) the Property
herein described was conveyed to the Husband and the Wife in fee
simple upon trust for themselves as beneficial joint tenants [subject as
hereinafter mentioned but otherwise] free from incumbrances

(B) By a Mortgage ('the Mortgage') dated   and made
between (1) the Husband and the Wife and (2) the Society the Property
was charged to the Society to secure the sum of £

(C) The sum of £   is now owing to the Society on the security of the
Mortgage

(D) The marriage between the Husband and the Wife having been
dissolved the Wife became the wife of *NH* on   at

(E) The Husband has agreed with *NH* for the sale to him of all his share
and interest in the Property and in the proceeds of sale thereof subject to
the Mortgage for the sum of £   and it has been agreed between the
Wife and *NH* that they should hold the Property subject to the Mortgage
as herein set out

(F) The Society has agreed to release the Husband from his obligations
under the Mortgage

NOW THIS DEED made in consideration of the sum of £   paid by
NH to the Husband (receipt of which the Husband acknowledges)
WITNESSES:

1 THE Husband and the Wife as trustees by direction of the Husband
directing as to ALL THAT his share and interest therein as beneficial
owner convey to the Wife and *NH* ALL THAT *etc* TO HOLD the same
to the Wife and *NH* as joint tenants in fee simple SUBJECT to the
Mortgage and all principal money and interest thereby secured [and

SUBJECT ALSO to the covenants and conditions mentioned in the conveyance so far as the same are still subsisting and capable of taking effect and affect the Property]

2 THE Society releases and discharges the Husband from his obligations under the Mortgage

3 *NH* covenants with the Society that he will pay to the Society all principal money interest costs and other monies due or to become due under the Mortgage and will observe and be bound by the agreements covenants and conditions contained or referred to in the Mortgage

4 THE Wife and *NH* declare that:
    (a) They hold the Property and its net proceeds of sale and the net income until sale on trust for themselves as tenants in common in equal shares
    (b) The trustees of this deed shall have all the powers of an absolute owner to deal with the Property

[5 *Covenant for indemnity if applicable—Precedent 34, clause 2*]

6 [*Certificate of value—Precedent 9, clause 7*]

IN WITNESS whereof this deed has been duly executed the day and year before written

Precedent 39—Registered Land

[*Same heading as Precedent 2*]

Date

1 In consideration of   pounds (£   ) paid by [*NH*] of
             ('NH') to [*Husband*] of   formerly of
             ('the Husband') (the receipt of which the Husband hereby acknowledges) We the Husband and [*Wife*] of   ('the Wife') as trustees by direction of the Husband directing as to all his interest therein as beneficial owner transfer to the Wife and *NH* the land comprised in the title above mentioned as beneficial tenants in common in equal shares SUBJECT to the Charge ('the Registered Charge') dated
             and registered on   under which there is now owing the sum of £

2 The   Building Society ('the Society') of
being the registered proprietor of the Registered Charge releases and discharges the Husband from all obligations under the Registered Charge

3 *NH* covenants with the Society that he will pay to the Society all principal money interest costs and other monies due or to become due under the Registered Charge and will observe and be bound by the

agreements covenants and conditions contained or referred to in the Registered Charge

[4 *Covenant for indemnity if applicable — Precedent 35, clause 3 substituting 'Husband' for 'Transferor'*]

5 [*Certificate of value — Precedent 9, clause 7*]

SIGNED [*see Precedent 34 with the addition of execution by the building society (Precedent 6)*]

D — Wife to receive whole property (in sole name of husband) by court order, but requests conveyance to self and new husband as joint tenants. No mortgage

Precedent 40 — Unregistered Land

THIS CONVEYANCE is made the   day of   19 BETWEEN (1) [*Husband*] of   ('the Husband') (2) [*Wife*] of   ('the Wife') and (3) the Wife and [*NH*] ('*NH*') of   (the wife and *NH* together called 'the Beneficiaries')

WHEREAS:

(A) [*Seisin of the Husband — Precedent 1, recital (A)*]

(B) [*Recital of Court Order — Precedent 1, recital (B)*]

(C) The Wife being entitled to the fee simple of the said property by reason of the Court Order has directed that the same should be conveyed to herself and *NH* and vested in them as joint tenants in manner hereinafter appearing

NOW pursuant to the Order and pursuant to the direction of the Wife THIS DEED WITNESSES:

1 THE Husband as beneficial owner at the direction of the Wife CONVEYS and the Wife as trustee CONVEYS AND CONFIRMS unto the Beneficiaries ALL THAT *etc* TO HOLD the same unto the Beneficiaries in fee simple [SUBJECT to the covenants and conditions mentioned in the Conveyance so far as the same are still subsisting and capable of taking effect and affect the Property]

2 THE Beneficiaries declare as follows: [*continue as Precedent 34, clause 3*]

3 THE Husband covenants with the Wife in the terms set out in Part I 2nd Schedule Law of Property Act 1925

[4 *Covenant for indemnity if applicable — see Precedent 34, clause 2 but substituting 'the Beneficiaries' for 'the Wife and NH'*]

5 IT IS HEREBY CERTIFIED that the transaction hereby effected

does not form part of a larger transaction or of a series of transactions in respect of which the amount or value or the aggregate amount or value of the property conveyed or transferred exceeds £60,000 [*Adjudication —see p 81*]

IN WITNESS *etc* [*execution by all parties*]

Precedent 41—Registered Land

[*Same heading as Precedent 2*]

Date

1 Pursuant to an Order of [Deputy] District Judge   in the   County Court dated   in proceedings between the Transferor and the Wife bearing number   and pursuant to a direction by the Wife to the Transferor

I [*Husband*] of   formerly of   ('the Transferor') as beneficial owner and by the direction of [*Wife*] of   ('the Wife') hereby transfer and I the Wife as trustee hereby transfer and confirm unto the Wife and [*New Husband*] of   (called 'the Transferees') the land comprised in the title above mentioned

2 The Transferor hereby covenants with the Wife in the terms set out in Part I 2nd Schedule Law of Property Act 1925

3 The Transferees declare that the survivor of them can give a good receipt for capital monies and that they are beneficial joint tenants

[4 *Covenant for indemnity if appropriate—Precedent 35, clause 3*]

5 [*Certificate of value—Precedent 40, clause 5*]

SIGNED [*execution by all parties*]

E—House in joint names of Husband and Wife. Wife entitled to Husband's interest by Court Order. Conveyance to Wife and New Husband. Mortgage. Husband released

Precedent 42—Unregistered Land

THIS CONVEYANCE is made the   day of   19 BETWEEN (1) [*Husband*] of   ('the Husband') (2) [*Wife*] of   ('the Wife') (3)   Building Society whose chief office is at   ('the Society') and (4) the Wife and [*NH*] of   ('*NH*') (the Wife and *NH* together called 'the Trustees')

WHEREAS:

(A) By a conveyance ('the Conveyance') dated   and made between (1)   and (2) the Husband and the Wife (the wife being then and in the Conveyance called [*Mrs H*]) the Property herein described was conveyed to the Husband and the Wife in fee simple upon trust for themselves as beneficial joint tenants [subject as hereinafter mentioned but otherwise] free from incumbrances

(B) By a Mortgage ('the Mortgage') dated   and made between (1) the Husband and the Wife and (2) the Society the Property was charged to the Society to secure the sum of £

(C) The sum of £   is now owing to the Society on the security of the Mortgage

(D) By an Order of [Deputy] District Judge   in the   County Court dated   in proceedings between the Husband and the Wife bearing number   the Husband was ordered to convey all his estate and interest in the Property to the Wife subject to the Mortgage

(E) The Wife being absolutely entitled to the Property subject to the Mortgage by reason of the Court Order has directed that the same should be conveyed to herself and *NH* and vested in them as joint tenants in manner hereinafter appearing

(F) The Society has agreed to release the Husband from his obligations under the Mortgage

NOW pursuant to the Order and pursuant to the direction of the Wife THIS DEED WITNESSES:

1 The Husband as beneficial owner in respect of his share and interest therein by direction of the Wife and the Husband and Wife as trustees CONVEY to the Wife and *NH* ALL THAT etc TO HOLD the same to the Wife and *NH* as joint tenants in fee simple SUBJECT to the Mortgage and all principal money and interest thereby secured [and SUBJECT ALSO to the covenants and conditions mentioned in the Conveyance so far as the same are still subsisting and capable of taking effect and affect the Property]

2 The Husband covenants with the Trustees in the terms set out in Part I 2nd Schedule Law of Property Act 1925

3 [*Release of Husband from Mortgage — Precedent 38, clause 2*]

4 [*Covenant by NH with Mortgage — Precedent 38, clause 3*]

5 [*Declaration as joint tenants by Wife and NH — Precedent 34, clause 3*]

6 [*Covenants for Indemnity if applicable — Precedent 34, clause 2*]

7 [*Certificate of value — Precedent 40, clause 5 — adjudication see p 81*]

IN WITNESS etc

Precedent 43—Registered Land

[*Same heading as Precedent 2*]

Date

1 Pursuant to an Order of [*Deputy*] District Judge   in the
                County Court dated   in proceedings
between the Transferor and the Wife bearing number   and
pursuant to a direction by the Wife to the Transferor We [*Husband*] of
                formerly of   ('the Transferor') and [*Wife*] of
                ('the Wife') as trustees with the Transferor directing as to
all his interest therein as beneficial owner transfer to the Wife and [*NH*]
of   ('*NH*') (the Wife and *NH* being 'the Transferees') the
land comprised in the title above mentioned SUBJECT to the Charge
('the registered Charge') dated   and registered on
                under which there is now owing the sum of £

2 The Transferor covenants with the Transferees in the terms set out in
Part I 2nd Schedule Law of Property Act 1925

3 The   Building Society ('the Society') of
being the registered proprietor of the Registered Charge releases and
discharges the Transferor from all obligations under the Registered
Charge

4 [*Covenant by NH with Mortgagee—Precedent 39, clause 3*]

5 [*Declaration as joint tenants—Precedent 35, clause 2*]

6 [*Covenant for Indemnity if applicable—Precedent 35, clause 3*]

7 [*Certificate of value—Precedent 40, clause 5—adjudication see p 81*]

Signed etc [*see Precedent 34 and Precedent 6 for building society*]

F—House in sole name of husband. Wife entitled to 50 per cent by court order. Sale of other 50 per cent to new husband. Wife and new husband to hold as joint tenants

Precedent 44—Unregistered Land

THIS CONVEYANCE is made the   day of   19
BETWEEN (1) [*Husband*] of   ('the Husband') (2) [*Wife*]
of   ('the Wife') (3) [*NH*] of   ('*NH*') and (4)
the Wife and *NH* ('the Trustees')

WHEREAS:

(A) [*Seisin of the Husband—Precedent 1, recital (A)*]

(B) By an Order of [*Deputy*] District Judge   in the
                County Court dated   in proceedings

between the Husband and the Wife bearing number   the Husband was ordered to stand possessed of the Property and the net proceeds of sale thereof as to 50 per cent for himself and 50 per cent for the Wife

(C) The Husband has agreed with *NH* for the sale to him of all his estate and interest in the Property and in the proceeds of sale thereof for the sum of £   and it has been agreed between the Wife and *NH* that they should hold the Property as beneficial joint tenants

NOW THIS DEED WITNESSES:

1 IN pursuance of the Order and in consideration of the sum of £ paid by *NH* to the Husband (the receipt of which the Husband hereby acknowledges) the Husband as beneficial owner by direction of the Wife as to all her share and interest therein and by direction of *NH* as to all his share and interest therein hereby purchased CONVEYS unto the Trustees ALL THAT etc TO HOLD to the Trustees in fee simple [SUBJECT (*continue as Precedent 1, clause 1*)]

[2 The Trustees covenant with the Husband to observe and perform the said covenants and conditions and to keep the Husband and his personal representatives effectually indemnified against all losses resulting from their non-observance or breach so far as aforesaid]

3 The Trustees declare that:
- (a) they hold the Property and its net proceeds of sale and the net income until sale on trust for themselves as beneficial joint tenants
- (b) the trustees of this deed shall have all the powers of an absolute owner to deal with the Property

4
- (a) It is certified that as regards the conveyance of the Property to the Wife this instrument falls within category H in the Schedule to the Stamp Duty (Exempt Instruments) Regulations 1987
- [(b) As regards the sale to *NH* it is hereby certified that the transaction hereby effected does not form part of a larger transaction or of a series of transactions in respect of which the amount or value or the aggregate amount or value of the consideration exceeds £60,000]

IN WITNESS *etc* [*see Precedent 34*]

Precedent 45—Registered Land

[*Same heading as Precedent 2*]

Date

1 Pursuant to an Order of [Deputy] District Judge   in the
                County Court dated   in proceedings
between the Transferor and the Wife bearing number   and
in consideration of   pounds (£   ) paid by [NH] of
                ('NH') to the Transferor the receipt whereof is hereby
acknowledged   I [Husband] of   formerly of
                ('the Transferor') as beneficial owner and by direction of
[Wife] of   and by direction of [NH] transfer to [Wife] and
[NH] ('the Transferees') the land comprised in the title above mentioned

2 The Transferees declare that the survivor of them can give a good
receipt for capital monies and that they are beneficial joint tenants

[3 The Transferees covenant with the Transferor to observe and
perform the covenants and conditions referred to in the Charges
Register so far as still subsisting and relate to the Property and to keep
the Transferor and his personal representatives effectually indemnified
against all losses resulting from their non-observance or breach so far as
aforesaid]

4 [Certificate of value—Precedent 44, clause 4]

SIGNED [see Precedent 34]

Chapter 6

Home to be Held on Certain Terms and Conditions

Whether the matrimonial home is held in the joint names of the husband and wife on trust for sale or is in the name of the husband alone, it is not unusual for the court to order that the house be retained but upon certain terms and conditions. Such an order may be made so as to ensure that there is a home for the children of the marriage. It may recognise that once the youngest child has left home the wife may again be able to take up gainful employment but that until that time she should be provided with a home rent free. It may also recognise that the husband should be entitled to a financial stake in the matrimonial home, such stake being made available to him at the end of the period specified in the court order or at a time previously agreed between the parties.

A typical court order (in this case the matrimonial home being in the husband's sole name) might be as follows:

> It is ordered that the Respondent do transfer the property known as 1 Blackacre Drive, Blackacre, to himself and the Petitioner (or to other trustees) to hold the same as to 60% for himself and as to 40% for the Petitioner. The Petitioner shall have the occupation of the property for herself and the children of the family to the exclusion of the Respondent upon the conditions set out in the form of the draft declaration of trust annexed. The property is not to be sold until:
> (i) (a) the youngest child attains the age of eighteen years
>   or
>   (b) the youngest child shall cease full time education
>   whichever is the later or
> (ii) the death of the Petitioner or
> (iii) the Petitioner shall remarry
> whichever shall first occur

94

The above type of order is commonly known as a *Mesher* order (after *Mesher v Mesher and Hall* [1980] 1 All ER 126), and whilst it has been criticised (see *Mortimer v Mortimer* [1986] 2 FLR 315) the court is still of the view that such an order might provide the best solution (see *Clutton v Clutton* (1990) *Times*, 14 November).

1 Comment on the Mesher order

Whilst this type of order is fairly common, it must be appreciated that it has defects as compared with an outright transfer of the matrimonial home to the wife. Certain facts need to be considered:

(i) *Repairs*—The court cannot expressly order a party to pay for or contribute towards the cost of repairs to the house the subject of the court order because its powers are limited to ordering periodical payments and lump sums. The preamble to the court order might indicate that it is made (for example) on the basis that the wife will keep the property in good repair; this is certainly 'persuasive' in the event of a row. Or, in the case of a consent order, the wife might undertake to pay for repairs. It is in the interests of both husband and wife that agreement be reached as to the responsibility for maintenance and repairs. In the absence of any agreement, or undertaking, then probably out of necessity the wife will have to pay for repairs, and explore the possibility when the trust comes to an end of applying to the court (under 'liberty to apply') for a variation of the division of the sale proceeds so that she is reimbursed.

In *Harvey v Harvey* [1987] 1 FLR 67 the house was held by husband and wife as trustees with provision for postponement of sale. The husband refused to cooperate in obtaining a second mortgage and improvement grant to deal with necessary repairs, and the court ordered the appointment of a Receiver of the husband's interest limited to those purposes.

(ii) *Changing house*—Most court orders relate to a specific property and do not make provision for the wife moving house and occupying another property upon similar terms and conditions. In the absence of any provision concerning this in the court order, the agreement/ declaration of trust made by the parties should seek to cover this.

(iii) *Ending of the court order period*—In practice, problems are now beginning to appear when one of the specified events happens (eg the youngest child attaining 18 years), for many court orders have provided who should pay outgoings and mortgage payments during the 'trust period' but made no provision thereafter during the period whilst the house is being sold. Again, this is something that should be covered in any agreement or declaration of trust.

Practitioners will also be aware of the difficulty in getting the wife out so that the husband can obtain his share of the proceeds of sale (see *Crosthwaite v Crosthwaite* [1989] 2 FLR 86).

(iv) *Charging Clause*—Specific provision should be made for this in the court order as the trustees (particularly if there are infants) cannot give themselves power to charge in the declaration of trust without authority.

(v) *Does there need to be a conveyance/transfer?*

Where agreement has been reached between the parties that the former matrimonial home be held upon terms similar to those set out in the court order it has been known (in a natural desire to save costs) for the agreement to remain based on correspondence between the parties or their solicitors, no other documentation being prepared. This is not satisfactory.

If the former matrimonial home was in the husband's sole name, then in the event of his death the wife has to prove her interest in it, and the correspondence will have to be unearthed to prove to the capital taxes office that, although the house is in the husband's sole name, his estate would not be beneficially entitled to the whole of the proceeds of sale. Further, a sale of the house in such circumstances cannot be arranged until a grant of representation to the husband's estate is obtained. The registration of a Class F Land Charge against the husband is not sufficient protection as the death of the estate owner brings this protection to an end (Matrimonial Homes Act 1983, s 2(4)).

If it is the wife who dies, her personal representatives may not be aware of her interest in the house or may have difficulty in producing proof of the same, much to the detriment of her estate.

Similar difficulties can occur if the former matrimonial home was in the names of husband and wife as beneficial joint tenants, for on the death of either it would appear to a purchaser that the survivor had the right to sell (Law of Property (Joint Tenants) Act 1964, s 1(1)).

In the event of the insolvency of either party, one would wish to be able to prove beyond doubt to a trustee in bankruptcy the interests of the parties in the property.

Where a court order is made, it is not sufficient for a copy of that to be placed with the title deeds with nothing further being done, for the court order can be misplaced or removed. In each case, therefore, the agreement between the parties or the court order should be properly carried into effect by way of a conveyance, severance, transfer or declaration of trust, the form of which is the subject of this chapter. As we have seen, the declaration of trust can deal with matters outside the court order, as long as both parties agree.

2 Procedure

Unless monetary payment is to pass from the wife to the husband (for instance, as in a case where the house is in the husband's sole name and the husband and wife agree that it is to be transferred to husband and wife and held by them upon certain trusts provided the wife pays the husband a sum of money—see Chapter 7), when the husband may require such money for his own purchase of another property, a contract between the parties would appear to be unnecessary. A court order enables either party to go back to the court if unreasonable delay in carrying out the terms of the order is experienced, and if there is to be a conveyance of the matrimonal home following an agreement between the husband and the wife (not incorporated into a court order) it is always open to either party to make application to the court at any time.

If the house was formerly in the sole name of the husband it would be quite appropriate for the wife's solicitors to insist on a full abstract of title commencing with a good root of title (although in practice it seems to be accepted that the title was properly investigated at the time of the husband's purchase); but in the case of a house already in joint names it is thought that this could be dispensed with, the wife's solicitor assuming that a proper investigation of title to the property was made at the time when the house was purchased by the husband and the wife.

The court may have ordered one party's solicitor to conduct the conveyancing; but if not so, it would seem appropriate (assuming the husband to be the conveyancing or transferring party) for the husband's solicitors, if the house is in the sole name or even if it is in the joint names of the husband and wife, to deliver to the wife's solicitors an epitome of title consisting of a copy of the last conveyance, copy of any mortgage, copies of any documents relating to 'sales-off' or other transactions affecting the property and copies of any covenants affecting the same. In the case of registered land, sufficient particulars of title or office copy entries of the same should be supplied to the wife's solicitors. It would then be for the wife's solicitors to draft the relevant conveyance/ transfer and declaration of trust (as appropriate) and submit these to the husband's solicitors.

Once the documentation is agreed it is suggested that a 'completion date' should be arranged so that the relevant searches can be made (see Chapter 3, p 30) and any payment of monies requisitioned in time for the 'completion date'.

3 Covenants for title

If the property is in the husband's sole name and is being conveyed to trustees (whether or not the trustees are to be himself and his wife or outside parties) upon the terms of the court order or the terms of the agreement reached between husband and wife, there seems no good reason, as mentioned in Chapter 3, why the husband should not convey 'as beneficial owner'.

As beneficial owner covenants are only implied where there is valuable consideration, the covenants (in the absence of such consideration) should be expressly incorporated by reference thereto in the conveyance or transfer.

4 Tax considerations

Chapter 2 has outlined the relevant tax provisions to be considered when the husband is disposing of his share or interest in the matrimonial home. In the cases that followed (ie the disposal of the whole of the matrimonial home to the wife (Chapter 3); a conveyance of the husband's interest in the matrimonial home to the wife (Chapter 4); and the conveyance of the husband's interest in the matrimonial home to a third party (Chapter 5)), once the husband had disposed of his interest no further tax considerations applied so far as the husband was concerned (unless there was an element of gift involved in the conveyance not at arm's length and the husband died within seven years, thus bringing in a charge to inheritance tax).

In the situations covered in this chapter, however, the husband is retaining an interest in the matrimonial home until the happening of a certain event. One must, therefore, bear in mind the tax which may become chargeable on the happening of such event. The creation of different interests in the matrimonial home (eg the right of the wife to have occupation thereof until the youngest child attains 18 years or until her death) would appear to create a settlement both for capital gains tax and inheritance tax purposes (*Booth v Ellard* [1980] 1 WLR 1443).

(a) Creation of the settlement

It is unlikely that the creation of the settlement will incur any liability to inheritance tax as being a transfer for value (Inheritance Tax Act 1984, s 3). Firstly, if the decree absolute of divorce has not been pronounced the parties are still husband and wife (*Fender v St John-Mildmay* [1938] AC 1); and we have seen that transfers between them (provided they are both domiciled in the UK) are exempt from a charge to inheritance tax (see Chapter 2, p 20) even if they are living apart.

Secondly, s 11 of the Inheritance Tax Act 1984 provides that a disposition is not a transfer for value for inheritance tax if made by one party to the marriage for the maintenance of the other party. This section gives relief in respect of a disposition made on the occasion of the dissolution of the marriage or if it varies a disposition made on that occasion. There is no definition of 'maintenance' in the Act.

Thirdly, if the marriage is dissolved the disposition may be one where no gratuitous benefit is intended (see Inheritance Tax Act 1984, s 10) as it is to settle the claim of the former spouse (see Chapter 2, p 20).

It is thought that, if the capital gains tax concession mentioned in Chapter 2 would apply should the husband have transferred the whole of his interest in the matrimonial home to the wife absolutely, it will also apply in these circumstances. No capital gains tax would, therefore, be incurred on the creation of the settlement. (Whitehouse and Stuart-Buttle, *Revenue Law*, 10th edn, Butterworths, para 37.74, supports this view.)

(b) Termination of the settlement

When the wife's interest in possession ceases (eg when the youngest child becomes 18 years of age) there should be no charge to inheritance tax on that part of the settled property that reverts back to the husband (Inheritance Tax Act 1984, s 53(3)) nor on that part which the wife receives (s 53(2)). If however, the husband dies before the wife (ie whilst her right of occupation subsists) his reversionary interest in the proceeds of sale is not excluded property and there will be a charge to inheritance tax (Inheritance Tax Act 1984, s 48(1)).

As far as capital gains tax is concerned, it is considered that the gain referrable to the wife's share in the house will be free from a charge to capital gains tax if the house throughout the term of the settlement has been the wife's only or main residence (Taxation of Chargeable Gains Act 1992, s 222). The husband would appear to be liable to capital gains tax on any increase in value of his share of the former matrimonial home between the date of the transfer into settlement and the date of the deferred sale. (The husband will not have occupied the property as his only or main residence nor is there a disposal between spouses—see Chapter 2.) However, the position is open to doubt where the husband has not elected that some other house should be treated for capital gains tax purposes as his main residence for the period. If the Revenue accept that the court order or agreement between the parties created a settlement on the ground that the interests of the beneficiaries are not of the same quality as the wife has a right of occupation (see *Booth v Ellard* [1980] 1 WLR 1443) Taxation of Chargeable Gains Act, 1992, s 225 provides that the gain accruing to a trustee on the disposal of settled property shall in effect be free from capital gains tax where during the period of ownership the house has been the only or main residence of the person entitled to occupy it under the terms of the settlement. It is thought that this might give relief to the husband for capital gains tax for the period from when the settlement is established (ie the court order or when the agreement between the parties was finalised) until its termination, but the application of this section to such a situation is not wholly clear. (See Whitehouse and Stuart Buttle, *Revenue Law*, 10th edn, Butterworths, §37.78.)

5 Form of the conveyance or transfer

(a) Unregistered land

If the house is in the husband's sole name it should be conveyed, for reasons mentioned earlier, to trustees who can be himself and the wife, or himself and an outsider, or not less than two outsiders (often one being nominated by the husband and one by the wife).

If the house is already in the joint names of the husband and the wife, then such tenancy, if held as beneficial joint tenants, should be severed and a memorandum of severance should be endorsed on the conveyance to the husband and wife (see Precedent 51). It is important to put a purchaser on notice that he will only get a good receipt if he pays any purchase money to two trustees or to a trust corporation (Law of Property Act 1925, s 27).

Following the spirit of the 1925 property legislation, the trusts relating to the house should be kept off the title. If the house is placed in the names of outsider trustees, then a separate declaration of trust should be made by them to evidence the terms upon which they hold the property. This is probably not necessary if the house is to be held by the husband and the wife as trustees upon the terms of a court order (which will be sufficient evidence in itself), but it is strongly advised if the house is to be held by the husband and the wife as trustees upon the terms of an agreement reached between them. Any potential problems will hopefully be settled whilst the terms of the declaration of trust are being agreed. As both the husband and the wife have an interest in the property, each should be provided with a copy of any declaration of trust.

Section 36 of the Trustee Act 1925 allows a surviving trustee to appoint a new trustee to replace (for instance) a trustee who has died. To protect both the husband and the wife (and their respective estates) any conveyance and declaration of trust might provide that any trustee appointed to replace the husband or wife should be appointed by their respective personal representatives. It would be prudent, to avoid argument, to have this expressly mentioned in any court order.

(b) Registered land

Any reference to a trust will be excluded from the register (Land Registration Act 1925, s 74). Therefore, a transfer from the husband to husband and wife 'to hold upon the trusts of a declaration of trust of even date' may be rejected by the registrar, for its wording puts him on notice of a trust the terms of which he does not know.

The legal title should be protected by the machinery provided by the Land Registration Acts, whilst the trusts should be contained in a separate declaration of trust made by the registered proprietors.

Where land is transferred to two or more proprietors, then (in the absence of a request for its exclusion) the registrar will automatically register a restriction to the effect that a disposition by a sole proprietor of land (not being a trust corporation) under which capital money arises will not be registered except under an order of the registrar or of the court (Land Registration Act 1925, s 58(3), Land Registration Rules 1925 (SR & O 1925 No 1093, r 213) and Land Registration Rules 1989, r 6).

It is probably better to go further than this, for the husband may die and the wife (by virtue of Trustee Act 1925, s 36) could appoint a new trustee malleable to her wishes and to the detriment of the husband's estate. It is, therefore, suggested that application be made to the registrar to enter a restriction under which no disposition is to be registered after the death of one of the proprietors without the consent of the personal representatives of the deceased proprietor (see Precedent 47). As in unregistered conveyancing, it would avoid argument if this is specifically mentioned in any court order. This additional restriction relates to any disposition and not just to those where capital monies arise. (Land Registration Rules 1989, (SI No 801) r 6.)

Obviously there must be evidence outside the registry of the trusts affecting the former matrimonial home and the declaration of trust set out at Precedent 50 is appropriate both for registered and unregistered land. Each trustee should have a copy.

6 Contents of the declaration of trust

The declaration of trust referred to in the previous section should contain not only the trusts upon which the former matrimonial home is held but in addition clauses relating to:

(i) *Repairs*—Outside trustees will particularly wish to ensure that they are under no obligation to see to the maintenance and repair of the property, and under no liability in respect of lack of maintenance and repair (see p 95).

(ii) *Changing house*—See p 95.

(iii) *Charging clause*—If any of the trustees are professional people (such as a solicitor) or such a trustee is likely to be appointed in the future, the trust document should contain the usual charging clause. (*see p 96*) If the trust is of the former matrimonial home alone, there will be no available cash out of which fees can be paid. During the life of the trust, it is unlikely that a professional trustee will actually have to do anything. The charging clause will enable him to collect fees at the end of the trust. The alternative, if it is contemplated that fees will be incurred during the life of the trust, is to take a separate deed of covenant from the husband and the wife, or either of them, whereby they or one of them agree to discharge the fees concerned.

(iv) *Infants*—If a child (or children) of husband and wife is to be a beneficiary at the end of the trust and is likely to be an infant at that time, the trustees should perhaps be given power to pay the child's share of the proceeds to the parent or guardian. The Trustee Act 1925, ss 31–32, should be extended (see *Williams on Wills* 6th edn, Butterworths, 1987, vol 2, p 1267 and 1275) if monies are to be retained until such child or children come of age, so that the trustees have flexibility in their use of both income and capital of a child's share of the trust fund, as should the power of investment so that it is not limited by the Trustee Investments Act 1961.

(v) *Insurance*—Section 19(1) of the Trustee Act 1925 limits a trustee's power to insure to insurance against fire to three-quarters of the value of the property; as the

E

trustees will probably not have any cash, the occupier wife should be made responsible for insurance. (see p 106).

7 Where the property is subject to a mortgage

In spite of the trusts imposed on the former matrimonial home or its proceeds of sale, the husband may remain liable in respect of any mortgage secured thereon, the intent being in effect that this should be deducted from or charged on his equitable share. Thus, if the house has to be conveyed or transferred to the husband and the wife as trustees, the building society will probably require the wife to covenant with the society in respect of the mortgage and the wife will require an indemnity from the husband in respect thereof.

If the house is already in the joint names of the husband and wife subject to a mortgage and the husband alone is to assume liability, then again the wife will require an indemnity from the husband. It is not likely that the mortgagee will release the wife as one of the owners of the legal estate from liability under the mortgage. Such indemnity can be contained in the declaration of trust to be made by the husband and the wife.

The necessity of obtaining consents to transfers subject to a mortgage from occupiers of the matrimonial home aged 18 years and over must not be overlooked in view of the effect of *Williams & Glyn's Bank Ltd v Boland* [1981] AC 487. (See Precedent 11.)

8 Steps to be taken following the completion of the conveyance or transfer and declaration of trust

(a) Stamp duty

Because it is considered that a settlement is created by each of the transactions contemplated in this chapter (see p 99) the documents concerned should be lodged (together with a copy thereof) for adjudication. The conveyance not being one of sale and not exactly within the provisions of the exempt regulations (see Chapter 2), stamp duty of 50p only will be payable (see p 24). A similar amount will be payable on any declaration of trust. No 'PD Form' will be required as there has been no conveyance or transfer on sale.

If the title is registered, any transfer should first be lodged at HM Land Registry (see Chapter 5, p 82, and Land Registration Rules 1925, r 95).

(b) Cancellation at HM Land Charges Registry or Land Registry

Any Class F Land Charge should be cancelled (Form K13—fee £1) as should any equivalent notice at HM Land Registry (Form 202, copy of decree absolute, no fee). Similarly it will be appropriate to cancel any pending action land charge (Form K11—fee £1) or any caution at the Land Registry (Form 71—no fee).

(f) Insurance

If the matrimonial home is in the sole name of the husband then it is best to change the insurance arrangements once agreement is reached or the court order made; the husband may neglect or to be unnecessary where the property already stands in the joint names of husband and wife and a separate declaration of trust is made. The copy of the court order should be kept with the declaration of trust.

Similarly, where the transfer has been pursuant to a court order, a certified copy of the order or marked abstract of the relevent portion should be lodged at HM Land Registry with the application for transfer.

(d) First registration of title

Unless any money is paid, such that there is a conveyance on sale of the whole of the property, it is not thought that any of the transactions in this chapter will involve a compulsory application for first registration of title (Land Registration Act 1925, s 123).

(e) HM Land Registry fees

The transfers in this chapter fall within the Land Registration Fees Order 1992 (SI No 2089). Fees are payable, on the basis of Sched 1, scale A, on the value of the land less charges secured thereon if there is a transfer of the whole and in the case of a disposition of only a share in the land on the equivalent proportion of the value of the land which is the subject of the dealing, after deducting therefrom an equivalent proportion of the amount secured on the land (by way of mortgage). Abatement 2(i) in

Sched 4, Pt I is available, reducing the fee to one-fifth (with a minimum of £40) if claimed when the transfer of the matrimonial home is made pursuant to a court order. The value of the land may be evidenced by a statement from the solicitors lodging the application (either by letter or on the Land Registry Form A4).

Where application is made for registration of a restriction only, Sched 3 of the Fee Order specifies a fee of £40. No fee is payable however if an application to register a restriction is accompanied by an application upon which a scale fee is payable.

(f) Insurance

If the matrimonial home is in the sole name of the husband then it is best to change the insurance arrangements once agreement is reached or the court order made; the husband may neglect or refuse to pay the premium, or worse, cancel the policy to obtain a refund. If the matrimonial home is transferred into the names of trustees, then it is best that the policy be in the name of the occupier of the property with the interest of the trustees being noted on the policy. This enables the occupier to submit a prompt claim to the insurers in the event of, for instance, a fire at the property.

(g) Leasehold

If the property concerned is leasehold, the requirements of the lease as to giving notice of any assignment should be observed.

PRECEDENTS

A—Conveyance of matrimonial home (in sole name of husband) to husband and wife to hold on terms of court order

Precedent 46—Unregistered Land

THIS CONVEYANCE is made the   day of   19
BETWEEN (1) [*Husband*] of   ('the Husband') and (2) the
Husband and [*Wife*] ('the Wife') of   (together called 'the
Trustees' which expression shall include all the other trustees for the
time being hereof)

WHEREAS:

(A) By a Conveyance ('the Conveyance') dated   and made between (1)   and (2) the Husband the Property herein described was conveyed to the Husband for an estate in fee simple [subject to the covenants and conditions as mentioned in the Conveyance but otherwise] free from incumbrances

(B) By an Order of [Deputy] District Judge   in the   County Court dated   in proceedings between the Husband and the Wife bearing number   the Husband was ordered to convey the Property to himself and the Wife to hold the same upon the trusts hereinafter mentioned

NOW pursuant to the Order THIS DEED WITNESSES:

1 THE Husband as beneficial owner [*see p 30*] conveys to the Trustees ALL THAT *etc* TO HOLD the same to the Trustees in fee simple [SUBJECT to the covenants and conditions mentioned in the Conveyance so far as the same are still subsisting and capable of taking effect and affect the Property]

2 THE Husband covenants with the Trustees in the terms set out in Part I 2nd Schedule Law of Property Act 1925 [*see p 30*]

3 THE Trustees declare as follows:
(a) The Trustees shall hold the Property upon trust to sell the same with power to postpone the sale thereof and shall hold the net proceeds of sale and other money applicable as capital and the net rents and profits thereof until sale upon the trusts set out in the Order and

(b) Until the expiration of 21 years from the death of the survivor of the Husband and the Wife the Trustees for the time being of this Deed shall have power to sell mortgage charge lease or otherwise dispose of all or any part of the Property with all the powers in that behalf of an absolute owner

[4 The Trustees covenant with the Husband to observe and perform the said covenants and conditions and to keep the Husband and his personal representatives effectually indemnified against all losses resulting from their non-observance or breach so far as aforesaid]

[5 The power of appointing a trustee in substitution for the Husband or the Wife following his or her death (as the case may be) shall be vested in their respective personal representatives]

[*Certificate of value not required—see Chapter 2, p 27—adjudication*]

IN WITNESS *etc*

Precedent 47—Registered Land

[*Same heading as Precedent 2*]

Date   Pursuant to an Order of [Deputy] District Judge
            in the   County Court dated   in
proceedings between the Transferor and [*Wife*] bearing number

1 I [*Husband*] of   formerly of   ('the Transferor') as beneficial owner hereby transfer to myself the Husband and
[*Wife*] of   (together called 'the Trustees') the land comprised in the title above mentioned

2 The Transferor covenants with the Trustees in the terms set out in Part
I 2nd Schedule Law of Property Act 1925 [*see Chapter 3, p 32*]

3 The Trustees hereby apply for the entry of the following restriction (in
addition to the usual obligatory restriction):

> Except under an Order of the Registrar no disposition by the
> proprietors of the land is to be registered after the death of any of
> the proprietors without the consent of the personal representatives of
> the deceased proprietor

[4 *Covenant for indemnity if applicable—Precedent 35, clause 3 substituting* 'Trustees' *for Wife and NH where appropriate*]

[*Certificate of value not required—see Chapter 2, p 27—adjudication*]

SIGNED as a Deed
by the said [*Husband*] in the presence of:

SIGNED as a Deed
by the said [*Wife*] in the presence of:

B—Conveyance of matrimonial home (in sole name of husband) to independent trustees to hold on terms agreed between husband and wife

Precedent 48—Unregistered Land

THIS CONVEYANCE is made the   day of   19
BETWEEN (1) [*Husband*] of   ('the Husband') and (2) [*X*]
of   and [*Y*] of   ('the Trustees' which expression shall include all the other trustees for the time being hereof)

WHEREAS:

(A) [*Seisin of the Husband—Precedent 46, recital (A)*]

(B) The Husband has agreed with [*Wife*] to convey the Property to the
Trustees and that the Trustees shall hold the same upon the terms set out
herein

NOW THIS CONVEYANCE WITNESSES:

1 THE Husband as beneficial owner [*see Chapter 3, p 30*] conveys to the Trustees ALL THAT *etc* TO HOLD the same to the Trustees in fee simple [SUBJECT to the covenants and conditions mentioned in the Conveyance so far as the same are still subsisting and capable of taking effect and affect the Property]

2 THE Husband covenants with the Trustees in the terms set out in Part I 2nd Schedule Law of Property Act 1925 [*see Chapter 3, p 30*]

3 THE Trustees declare as follows:
   (a) The Trustees shall hold the Property UPON TRUST to sell the same with power to postpone the sale thereof and shall hold the net proceeds of sale and other money applicable as capital and the net rents and profits thereof until sale UPON the trusts and with and subject to the powers and provisions declared of and concerning the same contained in a Declaration of Trust of even date and made between (1) the Trustees and (2) the wife [*insert parties as appropriate*]
   (b) Until the expiration of 21 years from the death of the survivor of the Trustees the trustees for the time being of this Deed shall have power to sell mortgage charge lease or otherwise dispose of all or any part of the Property with all the powers in that behalf of an absolute owner

4 THE power of appointing a trustee in substitution for [*X*] shall be vested in the Husband during his lifetime and after his death in his personal representatives and the power of appointing a trustee in substitution for [*Y*] shall be vested in [*Wife*] during her lifetime and after her death in her personal representatives

[5 *Covenant for indemnity if applicable—Precedent 46, clause 4*]

[*Certificate of value not required—see Chapter 2, p 27—adjudication*]

   IN WITNESS *etc*

Precedent 49—Registered Land

[*Same heading as Precedent 2*]

Date   1 I [*Husband*] of
formerly of
('the Transferor') as beneficial owner hereby transfer to [*X*] of
                and [*Y*] of   (together called 'the Trustees')
the land comprised in the title above mentioned

2 The Transferor covenants with the Trustees in the terms set out in Part I 2nd Schedule Law of Property Act 1925

3 The Trustees hereby apply for the entry of the following restriction (in addition to the usual obligatory restriction):

Except under an Order of the Registrar no disposition by the proprietors of the land is to be registered after the death of [X] without the consent of the Transferor or his personal representatives and after the death of [Y] without the consent of [Wife] or her personal representatives

[4 *Covenant for indemnity if applicable—Precedent 35, clause 3 substituting* 'Trustees' *for Wife and NH where appropriate*]

[*Certificate of value not required—see Chapter 2, p 27—adjudication*]

SIGNED *etc*

Precedent 50—Declaration of Trust (Registered or Unregistered Land)

THIS DECLARATION OF TRUST is made the   day of 19   by (1) [X] of   and [Y] of   (together called 'the Trustees' which expression shall include all other the trustee or trustees for the time being hereof) and (2) [Wife] of ('the Wife')

WHEREAS:

(A) By a Conveyance bearing the same date as but executed before this Declaration and made between (1) [*Husband*] and (2) the Trustees the freehold property known as 1 Blackacre Drive Blackacre was conveyed to the Trustees to hold the same upon trust for sale

[OR (if registered land)
(A) By a Transfer bearing the same date as but executed before this Declaration and made between (1) [*Husband*] and (2) the Trustees the freehold property known as 1 Blackacre Drive Blackacre registered at HM Land Registry with Title [Absolute] under Title No   was transferred to the Trustees]

(B) The Trustees make this Declaration to set out the trusts and the powers and provisions subject to which the said property is held

NOW IT IS HEREBY DECLARED as follows:

1 The following expressions shall have the following meanings:

(A) 'The dwelling' shall mean ALL THAT the property more particularly described in the Conveyance [Transfer] and any house bungalow flat or maisonette purchased by the Trustees in accordance with the provisions hereof in substitution for the said property

(B) 'The specified events' shall mean:
> (i) (a) the eighteenth birthday of [*A—youngest child*] who was born on   [*date*] or
>   (b) the date upon which [A] shall cease full time education whichever is the later or

(ii) the death of the Wife or
(iii) the re-marriage of the Wife
whichever shall first occur

2 The Trustees shall hold the dwelling UPON TRUST to sell the same but with the full power to postpone such sale

3 Without prejudice to the immediate binding trust for sale imposed by the preceding clause the Trustees may permit the Wife to reside in and continue to reside in the dwelling without payment therefor made by her to the Trustees and provided none of the specified events shall happen the Trustees shall permit the Wife to continue to reside in the dwelling until such time as she shall have signified to the Trustees in writing her wish no longer so to reside

4 As often as the Wife shall so request in writing the Trustees may at their discretion sell the dwelling currently held by them upon the trusts of the preceding clauses and with the net proceeds of sale purchase any other available dwelling designated by the Wife (but if such dwelling be leasehold only if the residue of the term of years granted by the lease exceeds 60 years at the date of such designation) the total cost of which (including all legal estate agency and survey fees and stamp duty and HM Land Registry fees if appropriate) does not exceed those proceeds (unless any excess shall be provided by the wife in which case such proportion of the future sale proceeds as such excess shall bear to the cost of purchase shall belong to the wife absolutely on any such future sale) and the Trustees shall hold such dwelling upon the trusts hereof but if on such substitution there should remain any surplus money in the hands of the Trustees they shall hold such surplus money upon the trusts of Clause 6 hereof

5 The Wife hereby covenants with the Trustees that for as long as she shall continue to reside in the dwelling she will pay the rent (if any) rates and other outgoings and keep the dwelling in good repair and insured comprehensively to its full value in an insurance office approved by the Trustees and in the joint names of herself and the Trustees and she shall within seven days of any demand being made produce to the Trustees or one of them such policy of insurance and the last receipt for premium in respect thereof and she will comply with all the terms and conditions affecting the dwelling as if she was the absolute owner thereof and was bound thereby and the Wife further covenants to indemnify the Trustees and each of them and their respective estates and effects against any loss damage liability charge or expense caused by or arising out of the failure by her to observe any of the terms and conditions aforesaid

6 Upon the happening of any one of the specified events the Trustees shall carry out the said trust for sale and shall stand possessed of the net proceeds of sale (which for the avoidance of doubt shall mean the sum

remaining after payment of all proper legal and estate agents' charges and disbursements in connection with the said sale):

    (i) as to 60 per cent for [*Husband*] or his personal representatives (as the case may be)

   (ii) as to 40 per cent for the Wife or her personal representatives (as the case may be)

and until such sale shall take place the Wife if remaining in occupation shall remain liable to pay the outgoings referred to in clause 5 hereof and keep the dwelling in good repair and insured as aforesaid

7 The Trustees and each of them shall be entitled to be indemnified out of the dwelling against all costs expenses damages claims and demands incurred or sustained by them by reason of their holding the dwelling upon the trusts hereof and in furtherance of such indemnity the Trustees shall be deemed to have all the powers (including the power of sale) given to a mortgagee under the Law of Property Act 1925 and shall be entitled to exercise the same to indemnify themselves or either of them under the provisions of this clause

8 (a) If after written demand made by the Trustees in that behalf the Wife shall have failed within a period of six weeks from the date thereof to put the dwelling in good repair or to insure the same as aforesaid the Trustees may in their entire discretion effect or cause to be effected such repairs as are necessary to put the dwelling into good repair or effect such policy of insurance and the Trustees and each of them shall be entitled to an indemnity in respect of any costs or charges incurred by them in so doing and in furtherance of such indemnity the Trustees shall be deemed to have the like powers to those set out in the preceding clause hereof PROVIDED ALWAYS that the Trustees shall not be liable to see to any such insurance or repair and shall be under no liability in respect thereof

(b) The Trustees may borrow money using the dwelling as security if required on such terms as to interest and repayment and otherwise as they may think fit for the purpose of carrying out such repairs as aforesaid

9 The power of appointing a trustee in substitution for [*X*] shall be vested in [*Husband*] during his lifetime and after his death in his personal representatives and the power of appointing a trustee in substitution for [*Y*] shall be vested in the Wife during her lifetime and after her death in her personal representatives

[10 *Charging clause if professional trustees:*
Any trustee hereof engaged in a profession or business shall be entitled to be paid all usual professional or other charges for business transacted and acts done by him or by a partner of his in connection with the trusts hereof (whether or not in the course of his profession or business)

including acts which a trustee not being in a profession or business could have done personally]

IN WITNESS whereof this deed has been duly executed the day and year before written

SIGNED *etc*

C—Matrimonial home (husband and wife joint tenants) to be held on terms of court order. Wife to repair and insure

Precedent 51—Unregistered Land

Memorandum [to be endorsed on last conveyance]

Memorandum Following an Order of [Deputy] District Judge   in the   County Court dated
and in proceedings between the within named [*Husband*] and the within named [*Wife*] bearing number   the joint tenancy in equity created by the within Conveyance between the said parties was severed

Precedent 52—Registered Land

Application to enter a restriction following Form 75

HM LAND REGISTRY
[continue heading as Precedent 2]

Date   We [*Husband*] of   and [*Wife*] of
hereby apply to the Registrar to enter the following restriction against the title above mentioned:

Restriction Except under an Order of the Registrar no disposition is to be registered after the death of either of the proprietors without the consent of the personal representatives of the deceased proprietor

SIGNED *etc*

Precedent 53—Declaration of Trust (unregistered and registered land)

THIS DECLARATION OF TRUST is made the   day of
19   BY [*Husband*] of   ('the Husband') and
         [*Wife*] of   ('the Wife')

WHEREAS:

(A) By a Conveyance ('the Conveyance') dated   and made between (1)   and (2) the Husband and the Wife the Property briefly described in the Schedule hereto was conveyed to the Husband and the Wife in fee simple as beneficial joint tenants

(B) Following an Order of [Deputy] District Judge   in the   County Court dated   in proceedings between the parties hereto bearing number   the joint tenancy created by the Conveyance was severed as the parties hereto hereby admit and it was ordered that the Property be held upon the terms hereinafter mentioned

[OR (A) The Husband and the Wife are registered as the proprietors at HM Land Registry of the property briefly described in the Schedule hereto on the basis that the survivor of them can give a good receipt for capital monies

(B) Following an Order of [Deputy] District Judge   in the   County Court dated   and in proceedings between the Husband and the Wife bearing number   it was ordered that the Property be held upon the terms hereinafter mentioned]

NOW IT IS HEREBY DECLARED as follows:

1 IN pursuance of the Court Order as from [*date of Court Order*] the parties shall HOLD the Property in fee simple UPON TRUST to sell the same and to stand possessed of the net proceeds of sale and the net rents and profits until sale in trust for the parties hereto as to [60] per cent for the Husband and as to [40] per cent for the Wife and otherwise upon the terms of the said Court Order

2 THE trustees hereof from time to time shall have power (until the expiration of 21 years from the death of the survivor of the Husband the Wife) to sell mortgage charge lease or otherwise dispose of all or any part of the said property with all the powers in that behalf of an absolute owner

3 The Wife covenants with the Husband that she will keep the Property in good repair and insured comprehensively to its full value in an insurance office approved by the Husband and in the joint names of herself and the Husband and she shall within seven days of any demand being made produce to the Husband such policy of insurance and the last receipt for premium in respect thereof

IN WITNESS *etc*

THE SCHEDULE
[*brief description of property from
title documents*]

D—Matrimonial home (husband and wife joint tenants) subject to mortgage, to be held on terms of court order. Husband responsible for mortgage

Precedent 54—Declaration of Trust—memorandum of severance (Pre-

cedent 51) or restriction (Precedent 52) having been completed
THIS DECLARATION OF TRUST is made the   day of
19   BY [*Husband*] of   ('the Husband') and
[*Wife*] of   ('the Wife')

WHEREAS:

(A) [*Recital of conveyance to Husband and Wife — Precedent 53, recital (A)*]

(B) By a Mortgage ('the Mortgage') dated   and made
between (1) the Husband and the Wife and (2) the
Building Society ('the Society') the Property was charged to the Society
to secure the sum of £

(C) The sum of £   is now owing to the Society on the security of the
Mortgage

(D) By an Order of [Deputy] District Judge   in the
County Court dated   in proceedings
between the Husband and the Wife bearing number   the
joint tenancy created by the Conveyance was severed as the Husband
and the Wife hereby admit and it was ordered that the Property be held
upon the terms hereinafter mentioned with the Husband being solely
responsible for the monies due under the Mortgage

NOW IT IS HEREBY DECLARED:

1 Pursuant to the Order as from [*date of Court Order*] the Husband and
the Wife shall hold the Property in fee simple UPON TRUST to sell the
same and to stand possessed of the net proceeds of sale (which for
the avoidance of doubt shall mean the sum remaining after discharge of
the Mortgage and payment of all proper legal and estate agents' charges
and disbursements in connection with the said sale) and the net rents and
profits until sale in trust for the parties as to   per cent for the
Husband and as to   per cent for the Wife SUBJECT to the
Mortgage and otherwise upon the terms of the Court Order

2 [*Powers of Trustees — see Precedent 53, clause 2 — unless these are
already contained in the original conveyance to the husband and wife*]

3 The Husband covenants with the Wife that with effect from [*usually a
date specified in the Court Order*] and until the Property be sold he will
pay and discharge all principal monies interest costs and other monies
secured by or henceforth to become payable under the Mortgage and
will at all times indemnify and keep indemnified the Wife and her estate
and effects against all proceedings costs claims and demands in respect
thereof

4 [*Covenant to repair — Precedent 53, clause 3*]

IN WITNESS *etc*

THE SCHEDULE
[*brief description of property from title documents*]

Chapter 7

Deferred Charges and Adjustment between Husband and Wife of their Interests

There are many adjustments that can be made to the interests of the husband and wife in the matrimonial home. It can be conveyed or transferred to one of them alone (see Chapters 3 and 4) or the rights of the husband can be postponed until the happening of a specified event (see Chapter 6). Similarly, the interest of one party can be increased (for instance, where the husband and wife hold the property as tenants in common and it is agreed, or ordered by the court, that the wife's share should be increased). Agreement should be reached on responsibility for repairs and insurance. More commonly, the parties (or the court) may consider that the matrimonial home should stand in the sole name of the wife but that the husband should be compensated by the payment of cash, or (if cash is not available) that the husband should have a charge on the property for a fixed amount (as opposed to an interest in the equity—as to which see Chapter 6), the calling in of the charge being deferred until a specific time or happening of a specified event (eg death of wife, remarriage of wife or youngest child attaining the age of eighteen years). Such an order, sometimes known as a *Browne v Pritchard* order (*Browne v Pritchard* [1975] 1 WLR 1366), might look as follows:

> It is ordered that the Respondent shall within 28 days transfer to the Petitioner the property known as 1 Blackacre Drive Blackacre and that the Petitioner shall thereupon execute a Legal Charge of the said property in favour of the Respondent in the form of the draft annexed to secure the sum of

£10,000 and that the said charge shall provide that the
statutory power of sale thereunder shall be deemed to arise
on the death or remarriage of the Petitioner or upon 10th
January 1999 whichever is the earlier.

From the husband's point of view it is obviously more satisfactory to have repayment of the mortgage on a fixed date or on the
happening of a specified event (such as remarriage of the wife) if
earlier rather than have repayment of his charge postponed until
sale of the property. In this latter event, unless he is to receive a
reasonable rate of interest on the monies outstanding, the monies
received on repayment of the charge could be worth very little in
purchasing power by the time they are received. Recognising this,
it is not unusual for the court to make an order that the property
be transferred to the wife, but with a charge in favour of the
husband equivalent to a percentage of the net proceeds of sale
with the calling in of the charge deferred until the happening of
one of the 'specified events'.

While the house in the wife's sole name with a fixed charge in
favour of the husband facilitates the wife's control of the
property, this does not offer her the flexibility to move house that
might be incorporated when the house is held by trustees until a
specified event (see Chapter 6). It is not appropriate to incorporate provisions to transfer the charge to another house in the
original charge, as the charge relates to a specific property, and
such provision should be contained in the consent order; such
flexibility can of course raise difficulties particularly if the wife
wishes to move down market and release some funds (without
repaying the husband) as this thereby reduces the husband's
security, especially if he only has the security of a second charge.

Very few court orders, whereby the husband is to take a charge
over the former matrimonial home, contain details of the specific
provisions to be contained in such charge. There is no reason why
a consent order should not incorporate a draft legal charge. If the
parties cannot agree on the terms of the mortgage, application can
always be made to the court who will settle the terms of the
mortgage or direct that conveyancing counsel be appointed by the
court to do so.

In view of the disadvantages of the husband having a fixed sum
tied up in property at a time of depreciating money values, practitioners might be advised to consider including in the mortgage a

provision to the effect that any capital sum received by the wife during the currency of the mortgage (for example, by way of inheritance or pools win) should be paid to the husband by way of reduction of the mortgage debt. It is suggested that such provision be specifically mentioned in the court order as it is unlikely to be accepted voluntarily.

Conversely, unless the charge so specifies, there is no limitation on the wife redeeming the mortgage early (*Popat v Popat* [1991] 2 FLR 163).

1 Conduct of the conveyancing

Unless any cash payment is passing which is required by the husband for the purchase of another property, a contract would appear to be unnecessary and is certainly not required if the transaction is to be carried out following a court order (whether by consent or otherwise) as application can always be made to the court for the terms of the order to be carried out (see Chapter 8).

As the wife is 'the acquiring party' it is appropriate that her solicitors should draw the appropriate conveyance or transfer and the husband's solicitors should, therefore, deliver a copy of the last conveyance, copies of any covenants affecting the title and copies of all 'sales-off' or other documents affecting the title since the last conveyance. In the case of registered title, office copy entries should be submitted to the wife's solicitors.

If the husband is to take a mortgage over the former matrimonial home, then, following usual conveyancing practice, his solicitors should draft and submit this to the wife's solicitors.

If the house was formerly in the sole name of the husband, it would be appropriate for the wife's solicitors to insist on a full abstract of title commencing with a good root of title, although it seems to be accepted in practice that the title was properly investigated at the time of the husband's purchase. If the house is already in the joint names of the husband and wife, it is usual to accept that the title was properly investigated at the time of purchase.

Once the documentation is complete, it is suggested that a 'completion date' be agreed, so that the necessary searches can be made (see Chapter 3, p 30) and monies requisitioned by reference to that date.

2 Covenants for title

There seems no good reason for the husband to be able to claim that he should not convey as 'beneficial owner' and the wife's solicitors should therefore insist that he so conveys (see Chapter 3).

3 Tax considerations

So far as the transfer of the property or the whole or part of the husband's share in it to the wife is concerned, the provisions set out in Chapter 2 apply and for the reasons there mentioned there is unlikely to be a liability for capital gains tax or inheritance tax.

Similarly the creation of a charge for a fixed amount in favour of the husband, and the repayment of that charge, would not appear to involve any liability for capital gains tax (Taxation of Chargeable Gains Act 1992, s 251 provides that there is no charge to capital gains tax on repayment of a debt to a creditor) or inheritance tax.

If the charge on the property in favour of the husband is not for a fixed amount but is expressed to be equivalent, for example, to one third of the net proceeds of sale, then the husband has acquired a chargeable asset (*Marren v Ingles* [1980] 1 WLR 983) and payment of the capital sum by way of redemption of the charge would appear to be a disposal for capital gains tax purposes (TCGA 1992, s 22). One would deduct from the amount received the value of the charge at the date the charge was executed in order to arrive at the taxable gain and claim other reliefs (see Chapter 2).

It is not thought that repayment of this type of charge would result in any charge to inheritance tax, as there is not a disposition intended to confer gratuitous benefit (Inheritance Tax Act 1984, s 10).

4 Form of the conveyance or transfer

(a) Unregistered land

If the house already stands in the joint names of the husband and wife as beneficial joint tenants and the wife is to have a specific interest therein, then the tenancy should be severed and a declaration of trust made (see Chapter 6). If, however, the husband and wife already hold as tenants in common, and there is to be an adjustment in the extent of their respective interests, then, so far as the legal title is concerned, no alteration needs to be made.

Any purchaser is already on notice that to get a good receipt he will have to pay purchase money to two trustees or a trust corporation (Law of Property Act 1925, s 27). However, the change in the equitable interests must be evidenced. To lodge a copy of the court order with the title deeds may be sufficient, but to be strictly formal a deed of assignment should be made. It is suggested that copies (or duplicates) be held by both husband and wife so as to evidence the extent of their respective interests.

On any assignment of an equitable interest, notice should be given to the trustees of the legal estate (*Dearle v Hall* (1828) 3 Russ 1); but if the husband and wife are the trustees this is academic. Notice should be given if the trustees of the legal estate are persons other than the husband or wife.

For the reasons mentioned in Chapter 6, the parties should be advised to agree how replacement trustees of the legal estate should be appointed, rather than the surviving trustee be left with this power (Trustee Act 1925, s 36). Such provision can be in a separate deed between the parties (to be lodged with the deeds). Agreement should also be reached as to responsibility for maintenance, repairs and insurance of the property (see Precedent 53).

So far as a transfer to the wife coupled with a deferred charge in favour of the husband is concerned, this should proceed by way of a conveyance/transfer (see Chapters 3 and 4) followed by a separate charge (see Precedent 62).

(b) Registered land

If the husband and wife hold as tenants in common, a restriction will already be on the register to the effect that a disposition by a sole proprietor of land (not being a trust corporation) under which capital money arises will not be registered except under an order of the Registrar or the Court (Land Registration Act 1925, s 58(3), Land Registration Rules 1925, r 213 and Land Registration Rules 1989, r 6). This restriction should be extended to protect the interest of the estate of either party by entering the further restriction set out in Precedent 52.

In addition, of course, there should be a Memorandum off the register or declaration of trust (see Precedent 53) as to the shares in the net proceeds of sale of each party, and obligations as to repair and maintenance.

(c) Property held by husband and wife and a third party

In circumstances where the husband is to convey his interest in the house to the wife, little needs to be done to the legal title other than for the husband to retire as a trustee; the wife and third party (possibly her mother) will be left holding the legal estate, the beneficial interests being 'behind the curtain'.

Section 39 Trustee Act 1925 provides that where a trustee desires to be discharged from the trust and where after his discharge there will be either a trust corporation or at least two individuals to act as trustees, then if the trustee by deed declares that he desires to be discharged and his co-trustees consent, he shall be deemed to have retired from the trust. (See Precedents 67 and 69.) The husband's beneficial interest will be dealt with by an assignment (Precedent 68).

5 Where the property is subject to a mortgage

If the matrimonial home is already subject to a mortgage then the requirements of the mortgagees will have to be ascertained prior to a conveyance or transfer and if, although the house is to remain in joint names, liability for the mortgage payments is to be assumed by one party, an indemnity to the other party will have to be included in the declaration of trust (see Precedent 54).

If the property is subject to a first mortgage and is, for instance, to be conveyed from the husband to the wife, subject to a charge being given in favour of the husband to secure a fixed sum, the husband will have to be satisfied with the security of a second charge, notice of which should be served on the first mortgagee. (See Precedent 64.)

It is not unknown for practitioners in a case where a second mortgage is to be given to incorporate the terms of that second mortgage in the conveyance to the wife. This is not wholly satisfactory, as often the terms of the second mortgage are not sufficiently clear for the husband to enforce them; it necessitates a separate form of receipt on redemption; and it leaves the husband effectively without any title documents (as these are held by the first mortgagee) although he can of course have marked abstracts.

Where the property is to be transferred subject to a mortgage, or where a new mortgage is to be created, it will be necessary to obtain consents to such transactions from any occupants of the property aged eighteen years or over (following the case of *Williams & Glyn's Bank Ltd v Boland* [1981] AC 487). (See Precedent 11.)

6 Steps to be taken following the completion of the conveyance or transfer

(a) Stamp duty

The circumstances envisaged in this chapter fall within s 83 of the Finance Act 1985 (see Chapter 2) and a certificate that the instrument falls within Category H of the Schedule to the Stamp Duty (Exempt Instruments) Regulations 1987 (SI No 516) can be given so that no stamp duty is payable.

A mortgage is not subject to stamp duty, the charge having been abolished (Finance Act 1971, s 64). A deed of appointment of new trustees (see Precedent 67) is also exempt from Stamp Duty).

Exemption A of the Stamp Duty (Exempt Instruments) Regulations 1987 will apply to Precedents 67 and 69 where, in contrast to Precedent 67, there is an actual transfer of land.

(b) Cancellation and registration at HM Land Registry: notices

If the former matrimonial home has been in the sole name of the husband, then on completion of the various transactions the Class F Land Charge (or notice if registered land) should be cancelled. Similarly, any registration of a pending action should be cancelled.

If any charge is given in favour of the husband and is subsequent to a first mortgage, then the husband should register a Class C(i) Land Charge (puisne mortgage) against the former wife and serve notice of the second charge on the first mortgagee (see Precedent 64).

As far as registered land is concerned, the second mortgage will be registered automatically against the title on the lodging of the application for registration. A second charge certificate will be issued to the husband, and the Land Registry will serve notice of the second charge on the first mortgagee (Land Registration Act 1925, s 30 as amended by Law of Property (Amendment) Act

1926, s 5) where the first charge was made for securing further advances (in addition to the original advance). The cautious practitioner might in any event serve notice of the second charge on the first mortgagee (see Precedent 64).

(c) Court order and completion of the abstract

In the case of unregistered land a copy of the court order or abstract thereof, marked as examined against the original, should be placed with the title documents.

In the case of registered land, a copy of the court order, marked as examined against the original, or an abstract of the relevant portion of the order so marked should be delivered with the application for registration of the transfer to HM Land Registry.

(d) First registration of title

Although the property may be in an area subject to compulsory registration of title no application is required unless the conveyance is one of sale (Land Registration Act 1925, s 123).

Even when equality money is paid by the wife (see Precedent 57) to the husband, the transaction would not appear to make registration compulsory as the dealing cannot be described as a sale. (See Ruoff and Roper, *Registered Conveyancing*, 1991 §11.07.)

If however doubts exist as to the application of the compulsory provisions, it is clearly wise to apply for registration *ex abundante cautela*.

(e) HM Land Registry fees

The registration or modification of a restriction (see p 121) will incur a fee of £40 (Land Registration Fees Order 1992 (SI No 2089)) although no fee is payable if the application is accompanied by an application upon which a scale fee is payable.

Unless the transfer is for a monetary consideration (in which case fees under Article 2, Scale A of the Order are payable) fees will be based, by virtue of art 2(5) of the Order, on the equivalent proportion of the value of the land the subject of the dealing after deduction therefrom of the equivalent proportion of the amount secured on the land. The value of the land may be evidenced by a statement from the solicitors lodging the application (either by letter or on HM Land Registry Form A4).

If claimed, and provided the transfer is made pursuant to an order of the court, advantage can be taken of Sched 4, Abatement 2(i) of the Order reducing the fee to one fifth with a minimum fee of £40.

Where a charge is given over registered land (eg Precedents 61 and 63), Scale 4 of the Fee Order will apply by reference to the amount of the charge. However, where a charge is delivered together with an application to register a transfer involving monetary consideration or before the application is completed, Sched 4, Abatement 1, provides that no fee is payable for the registration of the charge.

(f) Insurance

If the property passes to the wife alone, the insurance policy should be effected in her name. If the husband's name remained there, this could cause difficulties in respect of any claim as his receipt might be required.

If there is a mortgage granted in the husband's favour on the property, it is probably best either that the policy be in the names of the husband and wife, or (more properly) in the wife's sole name, but with the husband's interest as mortgagee noted thereon.

(g) Leasehold

Notice of assignment of leasehold property should be given to the lessor who should also be given details of any mortgagee so that, in the event of non-payment of rent, the mortgagee can be approached for payment, thus avoiding forfeiture of the lease.

*   *   *   *

PRECEDENTS

A — Assignment by husband (tenant in common) of part of undivided share in sale proceeds of matrimonial home to wife (other tenant in common) following court order. No sale until happening of specified event

Precedent 55 — Unregistered and Registered Land

THIS ASSIGNMENT is made the   day of   19
BETWEEN (1) [*Husband*] of   ('the Husband') and (2)
[*Wife*] of   ('the Wife')

WHEREAS:

(A) Under and by virtue of a Conveyance ('the Conveyance') dated and made between (1) [*XY*] and (2) the Husband and the Wife and of the Law of Property Act 1925 both the Husband and the Wife are respectively entitled to an equal half share of the net proceeds of sale of the Property herein described and the net rents and profits thereof until sale free from incumbrances.

(B) By an Order of [Deputy] District Judge   in the County Court dated   and in proceedings between the Husband and the Wife bearing number   it was ordered that the Husband and the Wife should stand possessed of the net proceeds of sale of the Property as to 75 per cent for the Wife and as to the remaining 25 per cent for the Husband and that the sale of the Property should be postponed until the happening of one of the events specified in the Order

NOW pursuant to the Order THIS DEED WITNESSES:

1 THE Husband as beneficial owner assigns to the Wife ALL THAT a one half share of the Husband's equal share of the net proceeds of sale and of the net rents and profits until sale [*leaving the Husband with a quarter share of the total thereof*] of ALL THAT *etc* [*parcels*] TO HOLD the same to the Wife absolutely so that henceforward the net proceeds of sale and the net rents and profits until sale of the Property shall be held as to 25 per cent for the Husband and 75 per cent for the Wife

2 THE Husband covenants with the Wife in the terms set out in Part I Second Schedule Law of Property Act 1925 [*see Chapter 3*]

3 THE Husband and the Wife agree with each other that no sale of the Property shall take place until the happening of one of the events specified in the Order and in accordance with the terms thereof unless both of them shall consent in writing thereto

4 [*Covenant to repair and insure by Wife—Precedent 53, clause 3*]

5 [*Stamp Duty Certificate—Precedent 1, clause 4*]

   IN WITNESS *etc*

B—Matrimonial home in husband's name. Conveyance to wife subject to payment. Court order

Precedent 56—Unregistered Land

THIS CONVEYANCE is made the   day of   19 BETWEEN (1) [*Husband*] of   ('the Husband') and (2) [*Wife*] of   ('the Wife')

WHEREAS:

(A) [*Seisin of Husband—Precedent 1, recital (A)*]

(B) By an Order of [Deputy] District Judge   in the
                  County Court dated   in proceedings
between the Husband and the Wife bearing number   the
Husband was ordered to convey the Property to the Wife for an estate in
fee simply upon receiving from her the sum of £[*4000*]

NOW in consideration of the sum of £[*4000*] paid by the Wife to the
Husband (the receipt whereof the Husband acknowledges) and in
pursuance of the Order THIS CONVEYANCE WITNESSES:

1 THE Husband as beneficial owner hereby conveys to the Wife ALL
THAT *etc* TO HOLD the same to the Wife in fee simple [SUBJECT
(*continue as Precedent 1*)]

[2 *Covenant for indemnity against covenants if applicable—see Precedent
1, clause 3*]

3 [*Stamp Duty Certificate—Precedent 1, clause 4*]

IN WITNESS *etc*

Precedent 57—Registered Land

[*Same heading as Precedent 2*]

Date   1 Pursuant to an Order of [Deputy] District Judge
              in the   County Court dated   in
proceedings between the Transferor and the Transferee bearing number
              and in consideration of   pounds (£   )
(the receipt of which is hereby acknowledged) I [*Husband*] of
              formerly of   ('the Transferor') as beneficial
owner transfer to [*Wife*] of   ('the Transferee') the land
comprised in the title above mentioned

[2 *Covenant for indemnity if applicable—see Precedent 2, clause 3*]

3 [*Stamp Duty Certificate—Precedent 1, clause 4*]

SIGNED *etc*

C—**Matrimonial home in joint names of husband and wife as
joint tenants. Transfer of whole to wife by court order.
Husband to have charge. Not to be called in until fixed date.
Interest payable meantime. Leasehold**

Precedent 58—Unregistered Land—leasehold

THIS ASSIGNMENT is made the   day of   19
BETWEEN (1) [Husband] of   ('the Husband') and (2)
[Wife] of   ('the Wife')

WHEREAS:

(A) By a Lease ('the Lease') dated   and made between (1)
[X] and (2) [Y] the property hereinafter described was demised by [X] to
[Y] for the term of [999] years subject to the rent thereby reserved and to
the covenants and conditions therein contained

(B) The premises demised by the Lease are now vested in the Husband
and the Wife as beneficial joint tenants for the residue of the term
granted by the Lease subject as aforesaid

(C) By an Order of [Deputy] District Judge   in the
          County Court dated   in proceedings
between the Husband and the Wife bearing number   the
Husband was ordered to transfer all his estate and interest in the said
property to the Wife absolutely

NOW pursuant to the Order THIS DEED WITNESSES:

1 THE Husband as beneficial owner RELEASES AND ASSIGNS to
the Wife ALL THAT the estate and interest of the Husband in ALL
THAT *etc* being the property comprised in and demised by the Lease
and the net proceeds of sale thereof and the net rents and profits thereof
until sale TO HOLD the same to the Wife for all the residue now
unexpired of the term of years granted by the Lease TO THE INTENT
that the Wife shall henceforth stand seised of the entirety of the said
property free from any estate or interest of the Husband therein and free
also from the statutory trusts SUBJECT henceforth to the payment of
the rent reserved by and to the covenants and conditions therein
contained or referred to in the lease and on the part of the lessee to be
observed and performed

2 [*Covenant for title—Precedent 3, clause 2*]

3 [*Stamp Duty Certificate—Precedent 1, clause 4*]

   IN WITNESS *etc*

Precedent 59—Unregistered Land—mortgage

THIS LEGAL CHARGE is made the   day of   19
BETWEEN (1) [Wife] of   ('the Mortgagor') and (2)
[Husband] of   ('the Husband')

WHEREAS:

(A) By a Lease ('the Lease') dated   and made between (1)
[X] and (2) [Y] the property described in the Schedule was demised by

[*X*] to [*Y*] for the term [999] years subject to the rent thereby reserved and to the covenants and conditions therein contained

(B) The premises demised by the Lease ('the Mortgaged Property') are now vested in the Mortgagor for the residue of the term granted by the Lease subject as aforesaid

(C) This Charge is made pursuant to an Order of [Deputy] District Judge   in the   County Court dated   in proceedings between the Mortgagor and the Husband bearing number   and wherein the Mortgagor was ordered to charge the Mortgaged Property in favour of the Husband to secure the sum of £[*4,000*] as herein set out

NOW pursuant to the Order THIS DEED WITNESSES:

1 THE Mortgagor covenants with the Husband to pay to the Husband [six] months from the date hereof [*this being the legal date for redemption*] the sum of £[*4,000*] with interest thereon from today at the rate of [12] per cent per annum and if such sum shall not be paid on that day then so long as any part thereof shall remain owing she will pay to the Husband interest at the said rate on the principal money for the time being hereby secured by equal monthly payments on the last day of each calendar month

2 PROVIDED that if (a) the Mortgagor pays interest at the said rate and on the said days (or within seven days of the same) and (b) the power of sale applicable hereto has not become exercisable and (c) the Mortgagor has complied with all her obligations hereunder then the Husband will not call in the said sum of £[*4,000*] or any part thereof before [*1 January 1997 or other specified event*]

PROVIDED ALWAYS that notwithstanding anything herein contained the power of sale applicable hereto shall be deemed to arise [six] months from the date hereof [**Note:** *this date will be the same as the legal date for redemption in clause 1*]

3 THE Mortgagor as beneficial owner CHARGES by way of legal mortgage ALL AND SINGULAR the Mortgaged Property with payment to the Husband of the principal money interest and any other monies hereby covenanted to be paid by the Mortgagor

4 THE Mortgagor covenants with the Husband that the Mortgagor:
(a) will at all times during the continuance of this security keep the Mortgaged Property in good and sufficient repair and condition and insured against fire and other risks in accordance with the covenants in that behalf contained in the Lease and if the Mortgagor shall be in default in the performance and observance of any of such covenants the Husband shall be entitled to repair and keep in repair the Mortgaged

Property and insure the same in accordance with the covenants and all money expended by the Husband under this power shall be deemed to have been properly paid by him

(b) will not during the continuance of this security without the consent in writing of the Husband register or cause to be registered under the Land Registration Acts 1925 to 1971 or any amendment thereto for the time being in force any person or persons as proprietor of the Mortgaged Property

(c) will not without the written consent of the Husband grant or agree to grant any lease or tenancy of the Mortgaged Property or any part thereof

(d) will on demand repay to the Husband all money properly paid and all charges costs and expenses properly incurred hereunder by the Husband together with interest thereon from the time of paying or incurring the same until repayment at the rate specified in clause 1 and until so repaid such costs charges and expenses shall be chargeable on the Mortgaged Property and shall be added to the principal money hereby secured with interest chargeable thereon at the rate aforesaid

(e) forthwith will produce to the Husband any order direction requisition permission notice or other matter whatsoever affecting or likely to affect the Mortgaged Property and served upon the Mortgagor and allow the Husband to make a copy thereof

(f) will pay to the Husband within thirty days of the receipt of the same any capital sum received by the Mortgagor (whether by gift inheritance or otherwise howsoever) by way of reduction of the principal sum hereby secured and for the purposes of this clause 'capital sum' shall be any sum in excess of £1,000

5 IT IS AGREED AND DECLARED that the statutory power of sale shall be applicable hereto with the extension following namely that the same shall become exercisable immediately by the Husband without notice to the Mortgagor if the Mortgaged Property or any part thereof or any chattel thereon belonging to the Mortgagor is taken in execution or if any chattel in the Mortgaged Property is taken under a distress for the rent reserved by the Lease

IN WITNESS *etc*

THE SCHEDULE before referred to
[*description of property in Lease*]

Precedent 60 — Registered Land — leasehold

[*Same heading as Precedent 2*]

Date   Pursuant to an Order of [Deputy] District Judge
            in the   County Court dated   in
proceedings between the Transferor and the Transferee bearing number   .

1 We [*Husband*] of   formerly of   ('the Transferor') and [*Wife*] of   ('the Transferee') as trustees and by direction of the Transferor directing as to all his interest therein as beneficial owner hereby transfer to the Transferee the land comprised in the above title for the residue of the term granted by the registered lease.

2 [*Covenant for title—Precedent 2, clause 2*]

3 [*Stamp Duty Certificate—Precedent 1, clause 4*]

SIGNED *etc*

Precedent 61—Registered Land—mortgage

HM LAND REGISTRY
[*Continue heading as Precedent 2*]

Date   Pursuant to an Order of [Deputy] District Judge   in the   County Court dated   in proceedings between the Mortgagor and the Husband bearing number   .

1 I [*Wife*] of   ('the Mortgagor') covenant with [*Husband*] of   ('the Husband') to pay to the Husband [six] months from the date hereof [*this being the legal date for redemption*] the sum of £[*4,000*] with interest thereon [*continue as Precedent 59*]

2 [*Take in Precedent 59, clause 2*]

3 The Mortgagor as beneficial owner CHARGES by way of legal mortgage the land comprised in the above title ('the Mortgaged Property') with payment to the Husband of the principal money interest and any other monies hereby covenanted to be paid by the Mortgagor

4 [*Take in Precedent 59, clause 4 referring to the 'Registered Lease'*]

5 [*Take in Precedent 59, clause 5*]

SIGNED *etc*

D—Matrimonial home in sole name of husband. Court order. Conveyance to wife subject to existing charge. Deferred charge in favour of husband for specific amount not to be enforced until certain events. No interest chargeable until happening of events

Precedent 62—Unregistered Land

THIS CONVEYANCE *etc* [*see Precedent 7*]

THIS LEGAL CHARGE is made the   day of   19

BETWEEN (1) [*Wife*] of   ('the Mortgagor') and (2)
[*Husband*] of   ('the Husband')

WHEREAS:

(A) By a Mortgage ('the First Mortgage') dated   and
made between (1) [*Husband*] and (2) [Blackacre Building Society] the
property described in the Schedule hereto ('the Mortgaged Property')
was charged in favour of the Building Society to secure the principal sum
and interest therein mentioned

(B) By an Order of [Deputy] District Judge   in the
                    County Court dated   in proceedings
between the Mortgagor and the Husband bearing number
the Husband was ordered to convey the Mortgaged Property to the
Mortgagor subject to the First Mortgage and the Mortgagor was ordered
to charge the Mortgaged Property in favour of the Husband to secure the
sum of £

NOW pursuant to the Order THIS DEED WITNESSES:

1 THE Mortgagor covenants with the Husband to pay to the Husband
[six] months from the date hereof [*this being the legal date for redemption
and when the power of sale arises*] the sum of £   with interest thereon
at the rate of   per cent per annum such interest only to become
chargeable with effect from the first of the dates below mentioned ('the
Specified Dates'):
     (i) the remarriage of the Mortgagor
     (ii) the death of the Mortgagor
     (iii) the eighteenth birthday of [*youngest child of the family*]
     (iv) [*a fixed date*]
such interest to be payable on the principal money for the time being
hereby secured by equal monthly payments on the last day of each
calendar month

2 PROVIDED THAT the power of sale applicable hereto has not
become exercisable then the Husband will not before the first to happen
of the Specified Dates call in the said sum of £   or any part thereof

PROVIDED ALWAYS that notwithstanding and without prejudice to
the provisions hereof the power of sale applicable to this Mortgage shall
for the protection of a purchaser be deemed to arise on [six] months
from the date hereof [*this will be the same date as the legal date for
redemption*]

3 THE Mortgagor as beneficial owner CHARGES by way of legal
mortgage ALL AND SINGULAR the Mortgaged Property with payment to the Husband of the principal money interest and other money
hereby covenanted to be paid by the Mortgagor SUBJECT to the First

Mortgage and the principal sum of £   and interest thereby secured

4 THE Mortgagor further COVENANTS with the Husband that the Mortgagor:

(a) will duly and punctually pay all interest payable in respect of the First Mortgage and will from time to time produce to the Husband on demand evidence of every such payment

(b) will at all times keep the Mortgaged Property insured in accordance with the covenant contained in the First Mortgage (whether or not the First Mortgage remains in force and effect) and produce on demand evidence of the terms of the policy and the receipt for the last payment of premium thereunder

(c) will at all times keep the Mortgaged Property in good repair and condition in accordance with the covenant in that regard contained in the First Mortgage

(d) will not charge the Mortgaged Property in favour of any person without the written consent of the Husband

(e) [*Covenant against registration — Precedent 59, clause 4(b)*]

(f) [*Covenant against leasing — Precedent 59, clause 4(c)*]

(g) [*Covenant to repay Husband's expenses — Precedent 59, clause 4(d)*]

(h) [*Covenant to produce notices — Precedent 59, clause 4(e)*]

(i) [*Covenant to reduce principal sum — Precedent 59, clause 4(f)*]

(j) will not borrow any further money on the security of the Mortgaged Property

5 IT IS AGREED AND DECLARED as follows:

(a) The statutory power of sale shall be applicable hereto with the extension following namely that the same shall become exercisable immediately by the Husband without notice to the Mortgagor

> (i) if the Mortgagor becomes bankrupt or has a Receiving Order made against her or enters into any arrangement or composition with her creditors;
> (ii) if a Receiver of the Mortgaged Property or any part thereof is appointed under the First Mortgage;
> (iii) if any step is taken or proceedings instituted by way of sale or otherwise for the purpose of enforcing the security constituted by the First Mortgage.

(b) The Husband may settle and pass the accounts of any person in whom the First Mortgage is for the time being vested and all accounts so settled and passed shall as between the Husband and his assigns and the Mortgagor be conclusive and binding on the Mortgagor

IN WITNESS whereof this deed has been duly executed the day and year before written

THE SCHEDULE
[*description of Mortgaged Property*]

SIGNED as a Deed
by the Mortgagor in the
presence of:

Precedent 63—Registered Land

HM LAND REGISTRY
[Continue heading as Precedent 2]

Date   Pursuant to an Order of [Deputy] District Judge
          in the   County Court dated   in
proceedings between the Mortgagor and the Husband bearing
number   .

1 I [*Wife*] of   ('the Mortgagor') covenant with [*Husband*]
of   ('the Husband') [*continue as Precedent 62*]

2 [*Take in Precedent 62, clause 2*]

3 The Mortgagor as beneficial owner CHARGES by way of legal
mortgage the land comprised in the above title ('the Mortgaged
Property') with payment to the Husband of the principal money interest
and other money hereby covenanted to be paid by the Mortgagor
SUBJECT TO the Charge dated   in favour of [Blackacre
Building Society] and registered on   ('the First Mortgage')

4 [*Take in Precedent 62, clause 4*]

5 [*Take in Precedent 62, clause 5*]

SIGNED *etc*

Precedent 64—Notice of Second Charge to First Mortgagee (unregistered or registered land—see p 122)

To [*name and address of First Mortgagee*]
Re [*Property*]
Your Account/Roll no

As Solicitors for and on behalf of [*Husband*] we hereby give you
NOTICE that by a Mortgage dated   and made between (1)
[*Wife*—*Mortgagor*] (2) [*Husband*] the above property presently in
Mortgage to you was charged by way of legal mortgage by the said [*Wife*]
to the said [*Husband*] to secure payment of the sum of £   and
interest

We request you to acknowledge receipt of this Notice by signing and
returning the duplicate hereof

Date
[*Name and address of Husband's Solicitors*]

E — Matrimonial home in sole name of wife (following court order) subject to existing charge. Deferred charge in favour of husband for percentage of sale proceeds on specified events. No interest chargeable meantime

Precedent 65 — Unregistered Land

THIS LEGAL CHARGE is made the   day of   19
BETWEEN (1) [*Wife*] of   ('the Mortgagor') and (2)
[*Husband*] of   ('the Husband')

WHEREAS:

(A) [Recital as to First Mortgage — Precedent 62, Recital A]

(B) By an Order of [Deputy] District Judge   in the
     County Court dated   in proceedings
between the Mortgagor and the Husband bearing number
the Husband was ordered to convey the Mortgaged Property to the
Mortgagor subject to the First Mortgage and the Mortgagor was ordered
to charge the Mortgaged Property in favour of the Husband to secure the
Specified Sum hereinafter defined

NOW pursuant to the Order THIS DEED WITNESSES:

1 In this Deed the following expressions have the following meanings:

    'the Repayment Date' shall be the first of the dates below mentioned:
        (i) the remarriage of the Mortgagor
        (ii) the death of the Mortgagor
        (iii) [*fixed date*]
        (iv) any disposition of a legal or equitable estate or interest in the
            Mortgaged Property
    'the Specified Sum' shall mean an amount equal to 25 per cent of the
net proceeds of sale of the Mortgaged Property after deducting
therefrom
        (i) the amount outstanding on the Repayment Date in respect of
            the First Mortgage
        (ii) any amount due to the Husband by reason of expenditure by
            him in accordance with clause 4(g) hereof
        (iii) the proper legal and estate agency charges and disbursements
            incurred in connection with the sale
OR in the event that the Mortgaged Property is not sold an amount
equal to 25 per cent of the amount that a qualified valuer appointed by
the Husband shall certify as the open market value of the Mortgaged
Property on the Repayment Date with vacant possession after
deducting therefrom the amount outstanding on the Repayment Date
in respect of the First Mortgage

2 The Mortgagor covenants with the Husband to pay to the Husband the Specified Sum on the Repayment Date with interest thereon at the rate of   per cent per annum from the Repayment Date until the date of actual payment

3 The Mortgagor as beneficial owner CHARGES by way of legal mortgage ALL AND SINGULAR the Mortgaged Property with payment to the Husband of the Specified Sum interest and other money hereby covenanted to be paid by the Mortgagor SUBJECT to the First Mortgage and the principal sum of £   and interest thereby secured

4 The Mortgagor further COVENANTS with the Husband that the Mortgagor:

(a) [covenant to pay First Mortgage—Precedent 62, clause 4(a)]
(b) [covenant to pay insurance—Precedent 62, clause 4(b)]
(c) [covenant to keep in repair—Precedent 62, clause 4(c)]
(d) [covenant not to charge—Precedent 62, clause 4(d)]
(e) [covenant against registration—Precedent 59, clause 4(b)]
(f) [covenant against leasing—Precedent 59, clause 4(c)]
(g) [covenant to repay the Husband's expenses—Precedent 59, clause 4(d) [substituting 'clause 2 for 'clause 1']
(h) [covenant to produce notices—Precedent 59, clause 4(e)]
(i) [covenant not to borrow further—Precedent 62, clause (j)]

5 [extension of statutory power of sale—Precedent 62, clause 5]

6 The power of sale and all other statutory powers vested in the Husband shall in favour of a purchaser arise [six] months from the date hereof

IN WITNESS whereof this Deed has been duly executed the day and year before written

THE SCHEDULE
[description of mortgaged property]

SIGNED as a Deed by
the Mortgagor in the
presence of:

Precedent 66—Registered Land

HM LAND REGISTRY
[Continue heading as Precedent 2]

Date   Pursuant to an Order of [Deputy] District Judge
          in the   County Court dated   in
proceedings between the Mortgagor and the Husband bearing
number   .

1 [Definitions — Precedent 65, clause 1]

2 [Wife] of   ('the Mortgagor') covenants with [Husband]
of   ('the Husband') [continue as Precedent 65, clause 2]

3 The Mortgagor as beneficial owner CHARGES by way of legal mortgage the land comprised in the above title ('the Mortgaged Property') with payment to the Husband of the Specified Sum interest and other money hereby covenanted to be paid by the Mortgagor SUBJECT to the Charge dated   in favour of [Blackacre Building Society] and registered on   ('the First Mortgage')

4 [Take in Precedent 65, clause 4]

5 [Take in Precedent 62, clause 5]

6 [Take in Precedent 65, clause 6]

SIGNED etc

F — Matrimonial Home held by Husband, Wife and Wife's mother as to two-thirds for the Husband and Wife as joint tenants and one-third for Wife's mother. Conveyance by order of court of Husband's interest to Wife

Precedent 67 — Deed of Discharge of Trustee — unregistered land

THIS DEED is made the   day of   19   BETWEEN (1) [Husband] of   ('the Husband') and (2) [Wife] and [mother-in-law] of   ('the Continuing Trustees')

WHEREAS:

(A) This Deed is SUPPLEMENTAL to a Conveyance dated made between (1) [Vendor to the parties] and (2) the Husband and the Continuing Trustees relating to Property details of which are given in the Schedule

(B) The Husband desires to be discharged from the trusts of the Conveyance

NOW THIS DEED WITNESSES:

1 The Husband declares that he desires to be discharged from the trusts of the Conveyance

2 The Continuing Trustees consent to the said discharge and the Husband is accordingly deemed to have retired as a trustee of the Conveyance

IN WITNESS whereof this Deed has been duly executed the day and year before written

SCHEDULE
[description of Property from last Conveyance]

[Attestation]

Precedent 68 — Assignment — unregistered and registered land

THIS ASSIGNMENT is made the   day of   19
BETWEEN (1) *[Husband]* of   ('the Husband') and (2)
[Wife] of   ('the Wife')

WHEREAS:

(A) The Husband and the Wife are entitled to a [two-thirds] interest in the Property and the net proceeds of sale thereof details of which are given in the Schedule

(B) By an Order of [Deputy] District Judge   in the
          County Court dated   in proceedings
between the Husband and the Wife bearing number   the
Husband was ordered to convey all his estate and interest in the Property to the Wife

NOW pursuant to the Court Order THIS DEED WITNESSES:

1 The Husband as beneficial owner ASSIGNS to the Wife ALL THAT his estate and interest in the Property and in the proceeds of sale thereof TO HOLD the same to the Wife absolutely

2 The Husband covenants with the Wife in the terms set out in Part I Second Schedule Law of Property Act 1925

3 It is certified that this instrument falls within Category H in the Schedule to The Stamp Duty (Exempt Instruments) Regulations 1987

IN WITNESS *etc*

SCHEDULE — 'the Property'
[details of the Property from last Conveyance or Land Certificate]

[Attestation]

Precedent 69 — Registered Land — transfer to give effect to discharge of trustee

[Same heading as Precedent 2]

Date   1 Pursuant to and to give effect to an order of
[Deputy] District Judge   in the   County
Court dated   in proceedings between *[Husband]* and
[Wife] bearing number   we *[Husband]* of
[Wife] of   and *[mother-in-law]* of   as trustees
transfer to *[Wife]* and *[mother-in-law]* of   ('the transferees')

the land comprised in the title above mentioned

The transferees declare that the survivor of them cannot give a valid receipt for capital money arising on a disposition of the land

It is certified that this instrument falls within Category A in the Schedule to The Stamp Duty (Exempt Instruments) Regulations 1987

[*Attestation*]

Chapter 8

Reluctance by Husband to Execute Conveyance

When the court has ordered that the husband should convey or transfer to the wife the matrimonial home (if in the husband's sole name) or his interest therein to the wife alone or to trustees, the situation increasingly arises where the husband either disappears without executing the conveyance or refuses or merely fails to execute it because he disapproves of the court order. We must consider how the wife's solicitors proceed in these circumstances. (In most such cases the husband will probably not have any solicitors acting for him, or if he has, those solicitors might find that they are unable to obtain meaningful instructions.)

If the matrimonial home is in the husband's sole name the wife's solicitors should in any event have taken steps to protect the wife's position by lodging an application for a pending action land charge (unregistered title) or an application for registration of a caution (if registered land) (see p 10) so that in effect the husband cannot deal with the property.

Most court orders contain a time limit (rarely, it must be admitted, adhered to) within which the husband must execute the conveyance or transfer. If no such time limit is imposed, then the order is defective; to avoid applying to the court asking it to make the order good by imposing a time limit, it is suggested that a reasonable period of time be allowed to elapse. By then the wife's solicitors should know if the husband has executed the document. Faced with the husband's reluctance or refusal to execute the document concerned, application can be made to the court for further help.

1 Vesting orders

It is often felt by those acting for the wife that if the court orders property to be transferred to her it should at the same time make a vesting order giving effect to its order for the transfer of property. It is supposed that not only will this save a further application to the court if the husband refuses to sign the conveyance but that costs will be saved as well.

Unfortunately, the legislation giving the court power to make vesting orders is not as far reaching as is commonly supposed.

The list of circumstances when a vesting order can be made is contained in s 44 of the Trustee Act 1925. The essence of the section is that there should be a trustee who fails to make the conveyance or transfer; and it is considered that once the court orders the husband to convey the matrimonial home or his interest in it to the wife, then the husband is constituted as a trustee for this purpose. Section 44(vi) provides that:

> Where a trustee jointly or solely entitled to or possessed of any interest in land, . . . has been required, by or on behalf of a person entitled to require a conveyance of the land or interest or a release of the right, to convey the land or interest or to release the right, and has wilfully refused or neglected to convey the land or interest or release the right for twenty-eight days after the date of the requirement

the court may make a vesting order vesting the land or interest therein in any such person in any such manner and for any such estate or interest as the court may direct.

Whilst the court can make a vesting order *ab initio* if the circumstances fall within the other provisions of s 44, in practice it prefers not to do so as it is a better exercise of justice to give the husband the opportunity of executing the conveyance himself. If he does not do so, and a vesting order is sought then it will be apparent that:

> (i) there must be evidence of wilful refusal or neglect by the husband to execute the conveyance or transfer (see Precedent 70);
>
> (ii) 28 days must have elapsed since the requirement should have been met;
>
> (iii) application will then have to be made to the court for a vesting order.

The county court can make a vesting order (Trustee Act 1925, s 63A as inserted by County Courts Act 1984, s 148(1) and Sched 2, Pt 1), but its power is limited to cases where the total value of the property involved does not exceed £30,000 (County Courts Jurisdiction Order 1981 (SI No 1123)). Where the value exceeds this figure, there would have to be a transfer to High Court jurisdiction; and whilst this is a matter of procedure it should be borne in mind.

It can be seen therefore that the legislation giving the court power to make vesting orders is not as far reaching as is commonly supposed; some orders are being requested which are a hybrid between a vesting order and something else.

There have for instance been attempts to 'telescope' the conveyancing by court orders declaring one of the joint proprietors to be deemed to be dead (see *Jones v Jones* [1972] 1 WLR 1269 where the Chief Land Registrar refused to register the wife as proprietor of the matrimonial home) or that 'the interest of the respondent in the matrimonial home be extinguished'. Such attempts do not work, quite apart from the fact that it is thought that a person can only be presumed dead after proper judicial process (see Matrimonial Causes Act 1973, s 19) and a registrar only has power to extinguish an interest in an *ante* or *post* nuptial settlement (s 24(1)(*d*)).

So far as registered land is concerned. HM Land Registry has power to give effect to vesting orders but such orders should contain a direction to the Chief Land Registrar and be clear and unequivocal in their terms. Sometimes the Land Registrar is unable to read into the court order an implied vesting order (see generally Ruoff and Roper, *Registered Conveyancing Looseleaf* edn, 1991, para 29.17 and Land Registration Act 1925, s 47(2)); and sometimes an order under s 39 of the Supreme Court Act 1981 or s 38 of the County Courts Act 1984 (see below) is put forward to HM Land Registry as a vesting order when really it requires to be put into effect by a conveyance or transfer.

Until, therefore, the scope of vesting orders is extended, it is thought safer in those circumstances where the husband refuses to execute a conveyance or transfer, or when he cannot be found, to make application to the court in the manner set out in the next part of this chapter.

2 Execution of the conveyance or transfer by the court

The court's power to execute a conveyance or transfer on behalf of a reluctant signatory or someone who is untraceable is contained in s 39 of the Supreme Court Act 1981 and extended to county court jurisdiction by s 38 of the County Courts Act 1984. As there is always the possibility that the husband will refuse to execute the conveyance or transfer, to save time and further application to the court, one is tempted to couple the original application seeking the transfer of property to the wife with a request that the court execute the relevant conveyance if the husband does not do so within a specified time limit.

Generally, the court will not make this latter order as it prefers to give the husband the chance to execute the document. The court does not like to presume that someone will disobey its order; and it is only likely to make such an order if the husband has shown by his past conduct that he certainly will not execute the document. Before the court gives its order as to execution it requires to be satisfied that the husband has neglected or refused to comply with its order (*Savage v Norton* [1908] 1 Ch 290).

In those cases where the court is satisfied that the husband will not execute the conveyance or transfer it may make an order further to the order for the transfer of property in the following terms:

> And it is further ordered that if the Respondent shall not have duly executed and returned to the Petitioner's Solicitors a proper deed of transfer of his estate and interest prepared by the Petitioner's Solicitors within the said 28 days or within 21 days of delivery of such deed of transfer to the Respondent's last known address at [*insert last known address*] (whichever shall be the later) then a District Judge of the County Court be appointed and authorised to execute the deed of transfer of the Respondent's estate and interest in place of the Respondent himself.

Whether or not the court makes this above further order it is suggested that following the order for transfer the wife's solicitors should send the engrossed conveyance or transfer together with a copy of the court order to the husband at his last known address by recorded delivery with acknowledgement of delivery being requested from the Post Office. If the conveyance or transfer is not received back from the husband duly executed within a reasonable time (or in the case of the court order above within the time-limit specified) application should be made to the court for the court to execute the conveyance or transfer.

In the usual case where the court had not anticipated that the husband would refuse to sign the conveyance, the order sought would be on the following lines:

> 1 An Order under Section 39 of the Supreme Court Act 1981 and Section 38 of the County Courts Act 1984 that a Conveyance to the Petitioner of the Respondent's estate and interest in [freehold] property at 1 Blackacre Drive, Blackacre shall be executed by such person as the Court may nominate for that purpose, the above named Respondent having failed or neglected to do so.
>
> 2 Such further or other Orders as may be just.
>
> [*3 Costs*].

A copy of the above application should be sent to the husband as before giving him details of the date, place and time of the hearing of the application.

The application should be supported by an affidavit giving evidence of the service of the court order directing the conveyance, upon the husband or to his last known address and evidence of the neglect of the husband to execute the same (see Precedent 70). Even if the court anticipated the husband's refusal to execute the conveyance it would want an affidavit showing that the husband had the opportunity to execute the conveyance; and the affidavit should therefore show that the conveyance was sent to the husband for execution together with a copy of the court order, or that both were served upon him.

The expected form of court order, following the husband's lack of response or refusal to execute the conveyance, would be as follows:

> The Court directs that the Conveyance to the Petitioner of the Respondent's estate and interest in 1 Blackacre Drive, Blackacre, be executed by a District Judge of the [   ] County Court.

The court order as to execution having been issued, or the court being satisfied in the case of anticipated refusal that the husband will not execute the conveyance, it will be necessary to re-engross the conveyance (as the husband will presumably still have this if his address is known or may have sent it back unsigned).

Whilst there is no reason why the conveyance should not be re-engrossed following the form of the document submitted to the husband for execution, it is strongly recommended that the practice of the relevant district judge first be ascertained. Although there can be no legal reason, owing to the overriding power of the court to execute the conveyance, it is known for a district judge to require a recital to the effect that the conveyance was served on the respondent husband who refused to sign the same. Similarly, it has been known for a district judge to refuse to execute a transfer giving the covenants for title contained in Precedent 19, clause 3 on the grounds that this was not a requirement contained in the original court order. To ascertain the individual requirements of the relevant district judge before re-engrossing the conveyance will thus save considerable time.

Following re-engrossment and subject to any particular requirements of the district judge, the conveyance can be lodged (by letter) with the clerk of the court with the request that it be placed before the district judge for his signature. On return of the conveyance duly executed by the court on behalf of the husband the steps following completion set out in previous chapters can be followed (as appropriate).

3 The lack of the title documents

We should consider the position where the title documents are not handed over or made available by the recalcitrant husband.

If the property is subject to a mortgage debt, no problem should arise, for the title documents will be under the control of the mortgagee and can be produced. If the property is not subject to a mortgage debt the situation is as explained below.

(a) Unregistered land

If it is known where, within the jurisdiction, the title deeds are, a court order would compel their production. A court order could be made (preferably at the same time as the order for transfer) that the documents of title be delivered up by the husband. The order should specify to whom the deeds must be delivered up.

If, however, the husband is outside the jurisdiction and the whereabouts of the deeds unknown, the wife's solicitors will have to proceed to prepare the conveyance on the basis that the title deeds are lost; the solicitors who acted on the purchase should be contacted to see if they have retained any relevant papers; statutory declarations should be made by the wife and previous owners (if available); and adjoining owners' solicitors should be contacted to see if any information can be given concerning covenants and the title generally built up so far as possible. Indemnity insurance should be considered. Registration of title should be applied for.

(b) Registered land

In the case of registered land, there is not the same problem of not being able to prove good title to a subsequent purchaser; for the title being registered, office copy entries of the register can be procured and a transfer prepared and executed.

The problem is that s 64 of the Land Registration Act 1925 requires production of the land certificate at the registry before registration of a dealing can be entered. Subsection (2) of that section gives the Chief Land Registrar power to compel production of the land certificate by summons under the seal of the registry. There is a fine on summary conviction which can be imposed on anyone having custody of the land certificate disobeying the summons (Land Registration Act 1925, s 128). In addition, the Chief Land Registrar has power under s 15 of the Act to require any person in whose custody the land certificate is to show cause why the land certificate be not produced; and penalties for non-compliance are set out. It is not thought, however, that these powers to compel production of the land certificate have ever been used; for it is understood that Land Registry take the view that if the husband is already defying a court order to sign a transfer, he is not likely to respond to an order requiring him to produce the land certificate.

The position is similar to that where the husband is outside the jurisdiction of the court and the whereabouts of the land certificate is not known.

It is thought that the present policy of the Chief Land Registrar in the case of a 'hard core' recalcitrant husband is to use the power under r 271 of the Land Registration Rules 1925 (SR & O 1925 No 1093) to issue a new land certificate, usually after service of notice and after the other provisions relating to lost or destroyed certificates have been followed (for the procedure, see Ruoff and Roper, *Registered Conveyancing*, Looseleaf edn, 1991, (para 3.37) and HM Land Registry Practice Leaflet No 3, November 1991).

* * * *

PRECEDENTS

Precedent 70—Affidavit of petitioner's solicitors where husband fails to execute conveyance. Mortgage

[*Order 20 Rule 10 County Court Rules 1981 (as amended by County Court (Amendment) Rules 1991 (SI No 525)) extending the practice direction dated 21 July 1983 ([1983] 3 All ER 33 relating to the Court of Appeal and the High Court to the County Court requires affidavits to be marked in the top right-hand corner, on the backsheet and on the front of any exhibit with details of (1) the party on whose behalf the affidavit is filed (2) the initials and surname of the deponent (3) the number of the affidavit in relation to the deponent (4) the date sworn (5) the date on which it is filed.*

Affidavits must not be bound with thick plastic strips or anything else which would hamper filing.

(1) *Petitioner*
(2) *W M Hartley*
(3) *1st*
(4) *3.12.90*
(5) *[Date of Filing]*

IN THE   COUNTY COURT

No of Matter

BETWEEN:

[*Wife*]   Petitioner
and
[*Husband*]   Respondent

AFFIDAVIT BY PETITIONER'S SOLICITORS IN SUPPORT OF APPLICATION FOR AN ORDER DIRECTING THE EXECUTION OF AN INSTRUMENT

I,   of
Solicitor, MAKE OATH and say as follows:
[*OR* following s 6 of the Oaths Act 1978 I,   of
     , solicitor, do solemnly and sincerely affirm and say as follows:]

1 That I am a Partner in the firm of   and that, as such, I have the conduct of this cause on behalf of the Petitioner.

2 That the Petitioner made application in her Petition herein for Orders, *inter alia*, transferring to her:

'Such interest if any as the Respondent has in the matrimonial home, 1 Blackacre Drive, Blackacre in the County of Blackacre'.

3 Notice of Intention to Proceed with the said application was duly given to the Respondent by post on [*date*] and, in due course the said application came for hearing before [Deputy] District Judge on [*date*] when he made the following Order:

'IT IS ORDERED that the Respondent shall transfer to the Petitioner absolutely within 28 days from the date of this Order all his estate and interest in the property at 1 Blackacre Drive, Blackacre'. Subject to the existing mortgage to the Blackacre Building Society, the Petitioner indemnifying the Respondent against all claims in respect thereof.

4 That I have in my possession, on loan from the Blackacre Building Society, mortgagees of the said property, the title deeds of the aforesaid property which deeds disclose that the said property is freehold and is vested in the joint names of the Petitioner and the Respondent as beneficial joint tenants subject to a Mortgage in favour of the said Building Society. Accordingly the only way in which the Respondent could properly and legally give effect to the said Order of the [Deputy] District Judge would be for him to execute a Conveyance of his said interest in the property to the Petitioner subject to the said Mortgage.

5 That my firm has drafted a Conveyance which said draft has been approved by the said Building Society. The engrossment of the said Deed is now produced and shown to me marked 'WMHI'.

6 That by letter dated   and sent by first class post, I wrote to the Respondent at his address as given to the Court at the aforementioned hearing, enquiring whether I should send the said Conveyance to him directly or to Solicitors on his behalf. I received no reply to my said letter.

7 That on the [*date*] my firm sent to the Respondent at the said address a letter by the Recorded Delivery Postal Service enclosing an engrossment of the said approved Conveyance and asking that the Respondent should execute the same and return it to me. The said letter, a copy of which will be produced at the hearing of this Application, also enclosed a copy of the said Order made by [Deputy] District Judge   My firm was notified by the Post Office Authorities that the said letter was delivered to the Respondent's address on the [*date*] but the said Deed has not been returned to me by the Respondent, nor has any reply to, or other acknowledgement of, the said letter been received.

8 That in the premises I can only conclude that the Respondent has failed or refused to execute the said Instrument which, by implication, the said Order of the [Deputy] District Judge directed him to execute and I therefore respectfully ask this Honourable Court to make an Order appointing some other person to execute the said Deed 'WMHI' in place of the Respondent.

9 That I submit that my means of knowledge sufficiently appear.

SWORN by the above-named
at   this   day of   19
[OR Affirmed at   this   day of   19   ]
Before me,

Solicitor
of the Supreme Court

This Affidavit is filed on behalf of the Petitioner
this   day of   19   by
                                        Petitioner's Solicitors.

Precedent 71—Affidavit by process server as to delivery of engrossed conveyance to husband and service of court order

[*For details of markings to be contained on Affidavits, backsheet and exhibits see head note to Precedent 70*]

(1) Petitioner
(2) J. Jones
(3) 1st
(4) 3.12.90
(5) [Date of Filing]

IN THE   COUNTY COURT
                                            No of Matter

BETWEEN:

                        [*Wife*]   Petitioner
                        and
                        [*Husband*]   Respondent

AFFIDAVIT OF SERVICE

I,   of
Process Server, MAKE OATH and say as follows:
[OR I,   of   Process server, do solemnly and sincerely affirm and say as follows:]

1 That I am instructed in this matter by Messrs
                        of
Solicitors acting for the Petitioner herein.

2 That on the instructions received as aforesaid I personally served the Respondent Husband at   o'clock on   day the   day of   19   at   with the following papers:

(a) a sealed copy of an Order of the Court dated the   a copy of which is now shown to me and marked 'JJ1';

(b) a Conveyance, a copy of which is now shown to me and marked 'JJ2';

(c) a letter addressed to the said Husband from Messrs   a copy of which is now shown to me and marked 'JJ3'.

3 That I know the person upon whom I served the aforementioned papers to be the said Husband because [I have previously served papers upon him for Messrs   and I beg leave to refer to my Affidavit sworn on the   as to the identity of the person upon whom I served the papers].

4 That I submit that my means of knowledge sufficiently appear herein.

SWORN *etc* [*see previous Precedent*]

Precedent 72—Attestation clause on conveyance to be executed by court

SIGNED as a Deed
by
a [Deputy] District Judge of the
County Court on behalf of
[*full names of Husband*] pursuant
to an Order dated the
day of   19   and made
under Section 39 of the Supreme
Court Act 1981 and Section 38 of
the County Courts Act 1984 in the
presence of:

Chapter 9

Life Policy Collateral to the Mortgage on the Home

1 Introduction

Although tax relief on life assurance premiums was abolished in respect of policies taken out after 13 March 1984 (Finance Act 1984, s 72(1)), increasingly mortgages on the matrimonial home are secured not only by a charge on that property but also by a charge on a life assurance policy which is assigned to the building society/mortgagee by way of collateral security. Some building societies are not insisting on formal assignments, and are content with the deposit of the policy with them (by way of equitable charge) and the service of a notice of deposit on the assurance company. When the mortgage is repaid no formal re-assignment of the policy needs therefore to take place; a notice of release of deposit is served on the assurance company and the receipted notice is placed with the policy. Some building societies (eg Halifax) have gone one step further: no assignment or deposit of the life policy is required, but if the policy is not kept up, the mortgage will revert to a repayment mortgage with revised monthly instalments to ensure its redemption by the end of the mortgage term.

The purpose of this chapter is not only to draw attention to the divorce practitioner that such policies may be in existence and should therefore be covered in the settlement between the parties in relation to the matrimonial home, but also to provide precedents as to how such policies may be dealt with.

It is important to appreciate that whilst the court can order the transfer of a policy, it cannot order a surrender, nor can it order a party to pay premiums. An undertaking contained in a court order can deal with either.

A typical court order may well be:

> It is hereby ordered that the Respondent do assign to the Petitioner within 28 days from the date hereof all his legal and beneficial interest in the policy of assurance effected with   Insurance Company under policy no   subject to the mortgage in favour of   Building Society.

2 Procedure

It is appropriate that the solicitor acting for the party who is to have the benefit of the policy should draw the deed of assignment and very often following the court order, the original policy is sent by the husband's solicitors to the wife's solicitors for them to draw the relevant assignment (unless the policy is subject to charge).

The original policy (or full copy) should be inspected so that:

(i) it can be checked that the terms of the policy are exactly as the parties thought and that the policy contains no unusual conditions or endorsements and is capable of assignment;

(ii) it can be ascertained that the age of life assured has been 'admitted' (ie the assurance company has seen the birth certificate of the life assured, lack of which can cause delay at the time of a claim).

The draft assignment can be submitted to the assignor's solicitors for acceptance together with a copy of the policy unless they retain the original until 'completion'.

It will be apparent that if the grantee of the policy is the husband alone and the agreement or order is that after repayment of the mortgage (ie the policy is to remain charged to the mortgagee) the husband is to have any surplus proceeds, then whether or not the matrimonial home is in the sole name of the husband (and is being conveyed to the wife) or in the joint names of the husband and wife (and is being conveyed to the wife alone), no deed of assignment of the surplus equity of the policy is necessary; once the mortgagee has repaid itself, it must account for the surplus policy proceeds to the policy-holder (ie the husband) or his estate.

As most life policies charged to a mortgagee are collateral to a mortgage of the matrimonial home, it is not considered necessary for the mortgagee to join in any assignment of life policy to release the husband from the charge affecting it if he is being released from the mortgage affecting the matrimonial home.

3 The different policies

(a) Policy on life of husband alone

Such a policy with the husband as the life assured and usually the grantee of the policy can be subject to an absolute assignment in favour of the wife (Law of Property Act 1925, s 136). Provided notice of assignment is properly given (see below p 158) the wife would be able to claim the policy proceeds on the death of the husband (producing the death certificate, the policy, the assignment and receipted notice thereof).

(b) Policies on lives of husband and wife

Such a policy will usually be written on the basis that husband and wife are the grantees of the policy with the monies payable on the death of the first of them to die, the surviving spouse (as surviving trustee) claiming the policy proceeds.

Under s 1 of the Policies of Assurance Act 1867, it would appear that an assignee of an equitable assignment is put in the same position as a legal assignee and thus in a position to claim the policy proceeds. The third edition of this book provided a precedent accordingly.

Leading insurance companies, however, take the view that they are not prepared to recognise such assignments, and assignments should accordingly be not only of the husband's equitable interest but of the legal interest of husband and wife.

The wife should consider whether or not she should appoint another trustee of the policy; if she were to die first, her surviving trustee could claim the policy proceeds without having to wait for a grant of representation to her estate (although such proceeds would be an asset of her estate).

(c) Policy under MWPA 1882 on husband's life for wife

A policy may have been taken out by the husband on his own life but written under the Married Women's Property Act 1882 for the benefit of his wife (often pre-1974 for estate duty reasons).

If the wife is to have the benefit of the policy, obviously no assignment need take place but there should be a change of trustee to avoid contact with the husband, should for instance the wife wish to surrender the policy. Under most trusts, the power of appointing new trustees is vested in the trustees for the time being (Trustee Act 1925, s 36). In the case of MWPA trusts, the power of appointing new trustees is vested in the life assured (MWPA 1882, s 11). Whilst in most cases this will be of little import, it could mean difficulty in appointing new trustees at a later date.

(d) Term policy in lieu of benefit from death in service

With the betterment of pension and death in service provision the wife (if the marriage had subsisted) could have expected to receive a substantial sum (often four times salary) in the event of her husband's death before pensionable age. Such sum is usually payable at the discretion of the trustees of the pension scheme guided by a memorandum of wishes signed by the husband.

In lieu of this, on divorce, agreement is often reached that the husband should effect term assurance until pensionable age and assign this to the wife, the husband paying the premiums. It is appropriate that if the wife should for any reason receive the death in service benefit she should pay those monies to her ex-husband's personal representative as she receives the policy proceeds. The inheritance tax position of such payment would have to be clarified at the time.

4 Covenants contained in the assignment

The covenants for title implied by the use of the words 'beneficial owner' are not limited to land alone (Law of Property Act 1925, s 76 and definition 205). As to the covenants implied see Chapter 3.

A beneficial owner covenant in relation to the assignment of a policy at the least provides the benefit of the covenant for further assurance (ie the assignor will put the title right). It is appropriate therefore for the assignee to insist that the assignor convey as beneficial owner.

For the reasons stated in Chapter 3 (ie no valuable consideration) it is prudent to expressly incorporate the beneficial owner covenants in the assignment.

In the precedents that follow other covenants are incorporated; the covenant contained in clause 2 should bring to the attention of the assignor that he should not undertake activities (such as motor racing) contrary to the terms of the policy; whether or not the assurance company would invoke the strict wording of the policy at the time of a claim is a matter of practice at that time.

5 Payment of premiums

Who is to pay the premiums is really a matter for the court order or agreement between the parties. For a pre-13 March 1984 policy on his life, the husband will continue to obtain tax relief on the payment of the premiums made by him (Finance Act 1984, s 72(1)). If the benefit of the policy on the life of the husband (subject to the existing charge) is to pass to the wife, then it is preferable that she should (subject to the question of tax relief —see above) have control of the payment of premiums. The payment of maintenance could be structured accordingly.

6 Steps to be taken following completion of the assignment

(a) Stamp Duty

The majority of assignments will fall within the provisions of s 83 of the Finance Act 1985 (see Chapter 2) and provided certificate H of The Stamp Duty (Exempt Instruments) Regulations 1987 (SI No 516) is endorsed thereon, no stamp duty will be payable.

If the assignment does not fall within the provisions of s 83, then it will be stampable *ad valorem* unless it contains a certificate of value (see Chapter 2).

The Deed of Appointment of New Trustees (Precedent 79) is not subject to stamp duty. (Finance Act 1991, s 110.)

(b) Notice of Assignment

Except in those cases where the husband is the grantee of the policy and is to remain entitled to the surplus proceeds, a notice of the assignment should be given to the assurance company and also to the building society/mortgagee so that surplus monies over and above those required to redeem the mortgage will be paid to the assignee. No assignee of a life policy can sue the insurance company for the policy monies until notice of assignment has been given and such notice should specify the date and purpose of the assignment. (Policies of Assurance Act 1867, s 3.)

* * * *

PRECEDENTS

Precedent 73—Policy on life of husband to be assigned to wife by order of court

THIS DEED OF ASSIGNMENT is made this   day of   19
    BETWEEN (1) [*Husband*] of   ('the Husband') and
(2) [*Wife*] of   ('the Wife')

WHEREAS:

(A) The Husband is entitled to the policy ('the Policy') details of which are set out in the schedule hereto

(B) By an Order of [Deputy] District Judge   in the
        County Court dated   in proceedings
between the Husband and the Wife bearing number   the
Husband was ordered to assign the Policy to the Wife

NOW THIS DEED WITNESSES:

1 The Husband as beneficial owner ASSIGNS to the Wife ALL THAT the Policy and all monies assured by or to become payable thereunder and all benefit and advantages thereof TO HOLD the same to the Wife absolutely

2 The Husband covenants with the Wife that the Policy is valid and in full force and effect and that he will not do or omit or knowingly suffer anything to be done as a result of which the Policy may become void or voidable or whereby the Wife or anyone claiming title through her may be prevented from receiving the monies thereby assured and all benefit and advantages thereof

[3 The Husband covenants with the Wife to continue to pay each and every premium due in respect of the Policy]

4 The Husband covenants with the Wife in the terms set out in Part I 2nd Schedule Law of Property Act 1925

5 It is certified that this instrument falls within Category H in the schedule to The Stamp Duty (Exempt Instruments) Regulations 1987

IN WITNESS whereof this deed has been duly executed the day and year before written

THE SCHEDULE

Assurance Company

Policy No

Life Assured   [*the husband*]

Sum Assured

When payable

Commencement of policy

Premium

SIGNED as a Deed
by the Husband in the presence of:

SIGNED as a Deed
by the Wife in the presence of:

Precedent 74—Policy on life of husband charged to building society to be assigned to wife (subject to charge) by order of court

THIS DEED OF ASSIGNMENT *etc* [*parties as Precedent 73*]

WHEREAS:

(A) The Husband is entitled to the policy ('the Policy') details of which are set out in the schedule hereto subject to a charge ('the Charge') thereon in favour of [*building society*] by an assignment dated   made between (1) the Husband and (2) [*building society*] [OR where policy is merely deposited by way of charge with building society (A). The Husband is entitled to the policy ('the Policy') details of which are set out in the schedule hereto subject to charge by way of deposit ('the Charge') in favour of [*building society*]].

(B) By an Order of [Deputy] District Judge   in the   County Court dated   in proceedings between the Husband and the Wife bearing number   the Husband was ordered to assign the Policy to the Wife subject to the Charge

NOW THIS DEED WITNESSES:

1 [Assignment—Precedent 73, clause 1] adding 'SUBJECT to the Charge'

2 [Covenant that Policy valid etc—Precedent 73, Clause 2]

3 [Covenant by Husband to pay premiums—if appropriate—Precedent 73, clause 3 *or* if Wife to pay premiums—Precedent 76, clause 3]

4 [Covenant for title—Precedent 73, clause 4]

5 [Stamp Duty certificate—Precedent 73, clause 5]

IN WITNESS etc [*see Precedent 73*]

THE SCHEDULE—see Precedent 73

Precedent 75—Notice of assignment to assurance company given on behalf of assignee

TO [*Assurance Company—name and address*]

Policy No

Life Assured

As Solicitors for and on behalf of [*Wife*] we hereby give you notice that by an Assignment dated   made between (1) [*Husband*] and (2) [*Wife*] the Policy above mentioned and all monies assured by or to become payable thereunder was assigned by the said [*Husband*] to the said [*Wife*] absolutely to give effect to an Order   of County Court dated   19   in proceedings bearing No   . [Subject to the existing charge in favour of [*Mortgagee*]]

   Please acknowledge receipt of this notice by signing and returning the duplicate hereof

Dated

SIGNED
[name and address of solicitors]

Precedent 76—Policy on lives of husband and wife charged to building society. Benefit of policy (subject to charge) by order of court to be assigned to wife. Wife to pay premiums

THIS DEED OF ASSIGNMENT etc [parties as Precedent 73]

WHEREAS:

(A) The Husband and the Wife are entitled to the policy ('the Policy') details of which are set out in the schedule hereto subject to a charge ('the Charge') thereon in favour of [*building society*] by an assignment dated   made between (1) the Husband and the Wife (1) and (2) [*building society*]

[OR where the policy is merely deposited by way of charge with building society

(A) The Husband and the Wife are entitled to the policy ('the Policy') details of which are set out in the schedule hereto subject to charge by way of deposit ('the Charge') in favour of [*building society*]]

(B) By an order of [Deputy] District Judge   in the   County Court dated   in proceedings between the Husband and the Wife bearing number   the

Husband was ordered to assign all that his right title and interest in the Policy to the Wife subject to the Charge

NOW THIS DEED WITNESSES:

1 The Husband and the Wife as trustees by direction of the Husband directing as to all his right title and interest as beneficial owner ASSIGN to the Wife ALL THAT the Policy and all monies assured by or to become payable thereunder and all benefit and advantages thereof TO HOLD the same to the Wife absolutely free from any estate or interest of the Husband therein SUBJECT to the Charge

2 The Husband covenants with the Wife that he will not do omit or knowingly suffer anything to be done as a result of which the Policy may become void or voidable or whereby the Wife or anyone claiming title through her may be prevented from receiving the monies thereby assured and all benefit and advantages thereof

3 The Wife hereby releases the Husband from any obligation to pay any further premiums in respect of the Policy and covenants to indemnify him from any liability under the Charge

4 [Covenant for title—Precedent 73, clause 4]

5 [Stamp Duty certificate—Precedent 73, clause 5]

IN WITNESS *etc*

THE SCHEDULE [see Precedent 73]

[Note Precedent 75 Notice of Assignment can easily be adapted to cover the notice required following the above assignment]

Precedent 77—Assignment by husband to wife of term policy to compensate for loss of death in service benefit. Covenant by wife to repay any benefit received from death in service scheme. Order of Court.

THIS DEED OF ASSIGNMENT *etc* [parties as Precedent 73]

WHEREAS:

(A) [Seisin of Husband—Precedent 73, Recital A]

(B) [Court Order—Precedent 73, Recital B]—and continue 'and the Wife was ordered to give the covenant hereinafter contained'

NOW THIS DEED WITNESSES:

1 [Assignment to Wife—Precedent 73, clause 1]

2 [Covenant that policy valid—Precedent 73, clause 2]

3 [Covenant by Husband to pay premiums—Precedent 73, clause 3]

4 [Covenant for title—Precedent 73, clause 4]

5 The Wife hereby covenants with the Husband that if following the death of the Husband the trustees of any pension or other scheme referable to his employment shall make payment to her of a capital sum she will hold such payment upon trust to pay the same to the personal representatives of the Husband subject to receiving an indemnity from them in respect of any taxation liability that might arise by reason of her payment to them

6 [Stamp Duty certificate—Precedent 73, clause 5]

IN WITNESS *etc* [see Precedent 73]

THE SCHEDULE [see Precedent 73]

Precedent 78—Policy on life of husband written under MWPA 1882 for benefit of wife. Husband as trustee. Benefit to be held for husband

THIS DEED OF ASSIGNMENT is made this   day of 19   BETWEEN (1) [*Wife*] of   ('the Wife') and (2) [*Husband*] of   ('the Husband')

WHEREAS:

(A) The Wife is entitled to the benefit of the Policy details of which are set out in the schedule hereto which Policy is held by the Husband as trustee for the Wife under the provisions of the Married Women's Property Act 1882

(B) By an Order of [Deputy] District Judge   in the County Court dated   in proceedings between the Husband and the Wife bearing number   the Wife was ordered to assign the benefit of the Policy to the Husband

NOW THIS DEED WITNESSES:

1 The Wife HEREBY ASSIGNS unto the Husband the benefit of the Policy and all monies assured by or to become payable thereunder and all benefit and advantages thereof TO HOLD the same unto the Husband absolutely

2 [Stamp Duty certificate—Precedent 73, clause 5]

IN WITNESS *etc*

SCHEDULE [see Precedent 73]

Note: No notice of assignment to the Assurance Company is necessary as the Husband is already the legal owner of the policy as trustee

Precedent 79—Deed of appointment of new trustees where MWPA policy on life of husband held for benefit of wife by husband and another who now retire as trustees

THIS DEED OF APPOINTMENT is made this   day of
19   BETWEEN (1) [Husband] of   ('the Appointor')
(2) the said [Husband] and XY of   (together called 'the
Retiring Trustees') and (3) [Wife] of   and AB of
     ('the New Trustees')

WHEREAS:

(A) The Retiring Trustees are the trustees of the policy ('the Policy')
details of which are set out in the schedule hereto effected by the
Appointor under the Married Women's Property Act 1882 for the
benefit of the Wife

(B) The Retiring Trustees being desirous of retiring as trustees of the
Policy the Appointor has determined to appoint the New Trustees to be
trustees thereof

NOW THIS DEED WITNESSES that in exercise of the statutory power
in that behalf and of every other power him enabling the Appointor
hereby APPOINTS the New Trustees to be trustees of the Policy in
place of the Retiring Trustees who hereby retire from the trusts thereof

IN WITNESS whereof this deed has been duly executed the day and
year before written

THE SCHEDULE—[See Precedent 73]

SIGNED as a deed *etc*

Precedent 80—Notice of assignment on appointment of new trustees of
a policy of assurance
TO [Assurance Company—name and address]

Policy No

Life Assured

As Solicitors for and on behalf of the trustees of the above Policy we
hereby give you notice that by a Deed of Appointment dated
     and made between (1) (2) and (3) [*as appropriate*] the said
(3) were appointed as trustees of the Policy in place of (2) who retired as
trustees thereof

Please acknowledge receipt of this notice by signing and returning the
duplicate hereof

Dated

SIGNED

[name and address of solicitors]

Chapter 10

The Insolvent Husband

1 Introduction

The purpose of this Chapter is to highlight a number of points relating to the matrimonial home, where there is potential or actual insolvency.

The possibility of the conveyance or transfer to the wife being set aside in the event of the husband's insolvency within five years of the date of the conveyance has already been mentioned (see Chapter 1 p 5). Such possibility should not of course discourage the court from making the order. (*Mullard v Mullard* [1982] 12 FLR 63.)

Of course, if the wife has notice of an act of bankruptcy on the part of the husband before any court order in her favour is made, she must expect the conveyance or transfer to be set aside.

The intermediate step could be a charging order (see Charging Orders Act 1979) against the husband's interest in the matrimonial home. That is almost a topic on its own and is not covered here; if the house is in the husband's sole name, the wife's right of occupation should be protected by the registration of a Class F Land Charge or registered notice equivalent (see Chapter 1) and if the house is in joint names, the wife should receive notice and her objection to the charging order application may well be adjourned so that it can be dealt with at the same time as her application for a property adjustment order (see *Austin-Fell v Austin-Fell* [1990] 3 WLR 33).

2 Insurance

It has already been mentioned (see Chapter 1) that the wife may be advised, at the time of the conveyance or transfer to her of the matrimonial home by the husband, to obtain a declaration of solvency from him; a purchaser from her within five years from the date of the conveyance/transfer may be concerned about the risk of the conveyance/transfer being put aside in the event of the husband's insolvency, and the declaration may help to allay the purchaser's concern.

Insurers would not appear to be providing insurance cover at the time of the conveyance/transfer to the wife against the risk of a transferring husband becoming insolvent within five years, but they do issue policies for a single premium providing cover to a purchaser from the transferee wife. The policy is usually written for the benefit of the purchaser, their mortgagees and successors in title (see for instance policies issued by Norwich Union).

Most insurance companies when providing insurance in favour of a purchaser/mortgagee in such circumstances require:

   (i) a copy of the matrimonial conveyance/transfer
  (ii) an up-to-date bankruptcy search against the transferor husband
 (iii) a copy of the conveyance to the purchaser
 (iv) a statutory declaration from the husband confirming solvency at the time of the conveyance/transfer to the wife *and* at the date the declaration is sworn.

Obviously if the husband has disappeared or refuses to co-operate insurance cover may not be available, and the purchaser (and his mortgagees) will have to take a view on whether or not the conveyance/transfer to the wife could be liable to be set aside. It is to be hoped that the statutory declaration referred to above taken at the time of the conveyance/transfer will in such circumstances be of persuasive effect.

3 The effect of the husband's insolvency on the ownership of the matrimonial home

(a) House in wife's sole name

One would assume that the wife's position as absolute owner of the matrimonial home was relatively unassailable if the husband becomes insolvent, unless of course there has been a transfer to her without consideration or at an under value within the last 5 years (see Chapter 1) and above.

A husband's trustee in bankruptcy may well however try to lay claim to an interest in the house (particularly if the husband has been paying the mortgage) and may either register a land charge at HM Land Charges Registry or lodge a caution at HM Land Registry which will not only stop the wife from disposing of the property but prevent her from raising monies on the security of it (Land Registration Act 1925, s 30(1)). The wife will receive notice of the caution and (if appropriate) should be prepared to oppose its registration (see Ruoff and Roper, *Registered Conveyancing*, Looseleaf edn, 1991, §36.17).

(b) House in husband's sole name

On the husband's insolvency title to the property automatically vests in the husband's trustee without conveyance (Insolvency Act 1986, s 306) subject to the interest of any mortgagee.

Prior to the enactment of the Insolvency Act 1986, the trustee could petition for sale of the house in the normal way and would not be bound by any rights that the bankrupt's spouse had registered under the Matrimonial Homes Act 1983. Section 336(2) of the Insolvency Act 1986 changes this and provides that where a spouse's rights of occupation under the Matrimonial Homes Act 1983 are a charge on the bankrupt's estate, the charge continues to subsist notwithstanding the bankruptcy.

Registration of her rights does mean that the wife is in a stronger position to negotiate for the purchase of the property from the husband's trustee.

(c) Joint Names

Where the matrimonial home is in the joint names of the husband and wife, legal title does not on the husband's insolvency pass to his trustee, because the property is already held on trust (Insolvency Act 1986, s 283(3)); the beneficial interest of the husband does of course vest in his trustee who, having a statutory duty to realise the bankrupt's estate, will invariably apply under s 30 of the Law of Property Act 1925 (see *Re Citro* (1990) *The Times*, 7 June) for a sale of the matrimonial home, unless an arrangement can be reached with the wife.

The beneficial joint tenancy of the matrimonial home is severed by operation of law where one party becomes bankrupt. Thereafter, husband and wife will hold as tenants in common in equal shares subject to any equitable accounting (see *Re Gorman* [1990] 1 All ER 717; where the trustee was entitled to an order for sale under s 30 but the court deferred such order to give the wife a chance to purchase the trustee's share).

Precedent 82 is designed to cover a situation where another member of the family provides money to buy out the bankrupt husband's equitable share.

A word of warning: sometimes the court is asked to make an order (where the house is in joint names of husband and wife) to transfer the husband's legal interest in the matrimonial home to the wife so that she can have sole conduct of a sale, from which the husband would receive something, sole conduct for the wife being necessary because of the husband's unwillingness to co-operate. Apart from the risk to the husband of the wife in such circumstances decamping with all the money, there is the possibility of the purchaser raising objection to the wife's title under s 339 of the Insolvency Act 1986. To avoid both difficulties, it is suggested that the husband retires as a trustee of the conveyance/title in favour of a new trustee (possibly his solicitor) so that the purchaser gets a good receipt for purchase monies (Law of Property Act 1925, s 37) from two trustees.

4 Steps to be taken following completion of the conveyance or transfer

(a) Stamp Duty

There will have been a conveyance or transfer on sale so that a PD Form will be required and stamp duty payable if the consideration exceeds £60,000; if it does not a certificate of value will be required.

(b) Completion of the abstract

A marked copy of the court order appointing the trustee in bankruptcy will be required to complete the unregistered title or for the purposes of HM Land Registry.

(c) First registration of title

An application for first registration of title will not be required unless the conveyance has been one of sale of the whole of the property (Land Registration Act 1925, s 123) (Ruoff and Roper, *Registered Conveyancing, Looseleaf* edn, 1991, §11.07)

(d) HM Land Registry fees

The purchase of the husband's share from his trustee in bankruptcy is a dealing for value within the Land Registration Fees Order 1992 (SI No 2089). Fees under Article 2 Scale A will be payable, based upon the amount or value of the consideration.

(e) Insurance

The appropriate changes should be made to delete the husband's name from the policy and add that of the sister-in-law (or other purchaser of the husband's share).

*   *   *   *

PRECEDENTS

A—Declaration of solvency by husband at time of conveyance/transfer to wife

Precedent 81—Registered land

I, [*Husband*] of   [*occupation*] and previously of [*address of matrimonial home*] do solemnly and sincerely declare as follows:

1 By a Conveyance/Transfer of even date herewith I have conveyed/transferred the property known as [*address of former matrimonial home*] to my former Wife [*Wife's full name*] following an Order of the   County Court dated   in proceedings bearing No

2 From an examination of my financial position at this date I have ascertained
    (a) that I have an excess of assets over liabilities and
    (b) that I am able to meet my debts and liabilities as they fall due
And as such I am solvent within the meaning of the Insolvency Act 1986

3 That I have never been adjudicated bankrupt and that to the best of my knowledge no bankruptcy proceedings are to be or have been commenced against me

And I make this solemn declaration conscientiously believing the same to be true and by virtue of the provisions of the Statutory Declarations Act 1835

DECLARED at
this   day of   19

Before me

Solicitor

B—Conveyance of insolvent husband's share of former jointly owned property (held as Beneficial Joint Tenants) to wife's sister who has provided the purchase price, the property being subject to Mortgage

Precedent 82—Unregistered Land

THIS CONVEYANCE is made the   day of   19
BETWEEN (1) [*name and address of Trustee in Bankruptcy*] ('the Trustee') (2) [*Husband*] of   and [*Wife*] of
('Husband' and 'Wife' respectively) (3) [Building Society] of
        ('Building Society') and (4) [*Sister-in-law*] of
[   ] ('Sister-in-law')

WHEREAS:

(A) By a Conveyance ('the Conveyance') dated   made between (1) [*previous vendor*] and (2) Husband and Wife the Property herein described was conveyed to Husband and Wife in fee simple upon trust for themselves as beneficial joint tenants [subject as hereinafter mentioned but otherwise] free from incumbrances

(B) By a Mortgage ('the Mortgage') dated   made between (1) Husband and Wife and (2) Building Society   the Property was charged to Building Society to secure the sum of £

(C) By a Certificate of Appointment of Trustee by creditors meeting registered in the   County Court bearing No
and dated   the Trustee was appointed Trustee of the Estate in Bankruptcy of the Husband

(D) The amount outstanding under the Mortgage is £

(E) The Trustee has agreed with Sister-in-law for the sale to her of all that the share and interest of Husband in the Property and the proceeds of sale thereof subject to the Mortgage for the sum of £   and it has been agreed between Wife and Sister-in-law that they should hold the Property subject to the Mortgage as hereinafter appears

(F) The Building Society has agreed to release the Husband and his estate in Bankruptcy from his obligations under the Mortgage

NOW THIS DEED made in consideration of the sum of £   paid by Sister-in-law to the Trustee (receipt whereof the Trustee hereby acknowledges) WITNESSES:

1 Husband and Wife as trustees by direction of the Trustee directing as to ALL THAT the beneficial share and interest of Husband therein CONVEY to Wife and Sister-in-law ALL THAT piece of land *etc* To HOLD the same unto Wife and Sister-in-law as joint tenants in fee simple SUBJECT TO the Mortgage and all principal money and interest thereby secured [and SUBJECT ALSO to the covenants and conditions mentioned in the Conveyance so far as the same are still subsisting and capable of taking effect and affect the Property]

2 Building Society releases Husband and his estate from all obligations under the Mortgage

3 Sister-in-law covenants with Building Society that she will at all times observe and be bound by the covenants and provisions of the Mortgage as if she had been a party to and executed the Mortgage as the 'borrower' therein

4 Wife and Sister-in-law DECLARE as follows:
    (a) they shall hold the Property and its net proceeds of sale and the net income until sale on trust for themselves as tenants in common in equal shares
    (b) the trustees of this deed shall have all the powers of an absolute owner to deal with the Property

5 The Wife and Sister-in-law covenant with the Husband to observe and perform the said covenants and conditions and to keep the Husband and his estate effectually indemnified against all losses resulting from their non-observance or breach so far as aforesaid]

6 It is hereby certified that the transaction hereby effected does not form part of a larger transaction or of a series of transactions in respect of which the amount or value or the aggregate amount or value of the consideration exceeds £60,000

IN WITNESS whereof these presents have been duly executed the day and year before written

[attestation by all
parties including the
Trustee and the Husband]

Precedent 83—Registered Land

[Same heading as Precedent 2]

Date

1 In consideration of   pounds (£   ) paid by [SL] of
              ('SL') to [TB] of   'TB' being the trustee of
the estate in bankruptcy of [Husband] receipt whereof TB acknowledges
              We Husband and [Wife] of   ('the Wife') as
trustees by direction of TB directing as to all Husband's interest therein
TRANSFER to the Wife and SL the land comprised in the title above as
beneficial tenants in common in equal shares SUBJECT to the Charge
('the Registered Charge') dated   and registered on
              under which there is now owing £

2 The   Building Society ('the Society') of
being the registered proprietor of the Registered Charge releases and
discharges the Husband and his estate from all obligations under the
Registered Charge

3 SL covenants with the Society that she will at all times observe and be
bound by the covenants and provisions of the Registered Charge as if she
had been a party to and executed the Registered Charge as 'the
borrower' therein

[4 Wife and SL covenant with the Husband to observe and perform the
covenants and conditions referred to in the Charges Register so far as
still subsisting and relate to the Property and to keep the Husband and
his estate effectually indemnified against all losses resulting from their
non-observance or breach so far as aforesaid]

5 [Certificate of value—see Precedent 82]

IN WITNESS etc—see previous precedent.

Chapter 11

Conveyance to Wife from Deceased Husband's Estate

From time to time, agreement is reached between husband and wife to the effect that if the matrimonial home is conveyed absolutely to the wife, she will seek no further financial provision from the husband, whether by way of capital or income, nor will she seek provision from out of his estate in the event of his death. Where agreement has been reached on this basis between the parties, it has been known for a conveyance to be made and expressed to be in full and final settlement of the wife's claims as indicated already. Naturally, when circumstances change, the parties seek advice as to whether or not this agreement can be upset.

It has long been held that the parties cannot by agreement oust the jurisdiction of the court. *Hyman v Hyman* [1929] AC 601 established that a spouse cannot by agreement give up the right to apply for financial provision in matrimonial proceedings and *Re M* [1968] P 174 held that an agreement between husband and wife that the wife would not make application for provision out of the husband's estate did not oust the jurisdiction of the court to make such provision.

In short, therefore, any agreement between the parties to the extent mentioned above will be ineffective in barring the jurisdiction of the court.

1 Avoiding further claims against the husband during his lifetime

The case of *L v L* [1962] P 101 established that an agreement between the parties that the wife would not seek further financial provision in matrimonial proceedings from the husband could only be effective if sanctioned by the court (see further *Minton v Minton* [1979] 2 WLR 31).

The advantages of a court order, where final agreement is reached between the parties, has been mentioned earlier (see p 2). In view of the encouragement now given to the principle of the 'clean break' by the provisions of the Matrimonial and Family Proceedings Act 1984, it is certainly in the husband's interest (in the context of this book) to seek a court order where financial matters between himself and his wife are settled by agreement and the aim must be to achieve a court order as follows:

> that the terms of the order are in full and final settlement of all claims which each party may have against the other, whether pursuant to the Matrimonial Causes Act 1973, the Married Women's Property Act 1882 or otherwise howsoever.

A conveyance expressed to be in full and final settlement of the wife's claim in the absence of a court order does not, as seen above, bar future application to the court, and at best such expression can only be evidentiary.

2 Avoiding a claim against the husband's estate after his death

Just as the conveyance of the matrimonial home to the wife may, with the consent of the court, stop further applications by her against the former husband during his lifetime, so too, with the consent of the court, can applications by the former wife against the former husband's estate after his death be avoided.

The Inheritance (Provision for Family and Dependants) Act 1975 which came into operation in respect of deaths occurring after 1 April 1976, allows any member of a specified class of persons to apply to the court on the grounds that the disposition of the deceased's estate is not such as to make reasonable financial provision for the applicant (s 1(1)) provided the deceased died domiciled in England or Wales.

Amongst the specified class are a spouse and a former wife or husband of the deceased who has not remarried (s 1(1)(b)). But even if the former spouse has remarried a claim can be made under the provisions of s 1(1)(e) if immediately before the death the applicant was being maintained either wholly or partly by the deceased.

The husband, therefore, in making financial settlement with the wife, will wish to ensure that she cannot claim against his estate. Section 15 of the Act provides that, on the granting of a decree of divorce, the court, with the agreement of the parties, and if it considers it appropriate can order that either party be precluded from applying against the estate of the other under the provisions of this Act.

A court order, under s 15 may be as follows:

> Pursuant to Section 15(1) of the Inheritance (Provision for Family and Dependants) Act 1975 neither party shall upon the death of the other be entitled to make a claim for an order under Section 2 of that Act the court considering it just so to order.

Section 2 sets out the type of orders that the court may make in respect of the deceased's estate.

It is suggested that a copy of such court order be placed with the will of the party in whose benefit it is made so that his executors are in a position quickly to rebut a claim of a former spouse.

Prior to the passing of the Inheritance (Provision for Family and Dependants) Act 1975 there were several devices employed for avoiding the claim of a spouse against the other's estate. The present position is fully discussed in *Williams on Wills* 6th edn, Chapter 102 and s 10 of the Act.

3 Conveyance to wife following proceedings under Inheritance (Provision for Family and Dependants) Act 1975

If, however, the wife is not barred from claiming against the estate of the former husband, she may bring proceedings against that estate under this Act. By virtue of s 2(1)(c) the court has power to make an order for the transfer to the applicant of property comprised in the estate.

In deciding what provision is reasonable for the surviving spouse, the court must ask itself the question 'what would a family judge have ordered for this couple if divorce instead of death had divided them'? (*Moody v Stevenson* [1991] *The Times*, 30 July).

It is worth noting that a transfer of a dwelling house pursuant to an order under s 2 does not trigger the repayment of any discount granted in respect of a house purchased by the deceased under the provisions of the Housing Act 1985 from the Local Authority (Housing Act 1985, s 39(1)(c)).

(a) Unregistered land

The court may direct an outright transfer to the wife of the former husband's interest in the matrimonial home, whether it be in the sole name of the husband or in the names of the husband and wife as tenants in common.

Alternatively, it may direct that the house be held upon certain trusts; for instance, for the wife for life and after her death upon the terms of the husband's will. In such a case, the house should be conveyed to trustees to hold the same upon the terms of the court order (Precedent 46 can be adapted to this).

If the house is already in the joint names of husband and wife, who held as tenants in common, then strictly all the wife need do is appoint another trustee of the conveyance (Trustee Act 1925, s 36) to act with herself. On any sale a purchaser would get a good receipt if the purchase monies were paid to either two trustees or a trust corporation (Law of Property Act 1925, s 27(2)); such purchaser need not concern himself with the trusts upon which the monies are held. It is obviously advisable, from the point of view of the husband's estate for the other trustee of the conveyance to be one of the husband's personal representatives, and in any proceedings under the inheritance provisions this should be requested, coupled with a request for a direction that future replacements for the 'husband's trustee' be appointed by his personal representatives (see, for example, Precedent 48).

(b) Registered land

If the husband and wife held the land as tenants in common there will be already a restriction on the register to the effect that a disposition by a sole proprietor of land (not being a trust corporation) under which capital money arises will not be registered except under an order of the registrar or of the court (Land Registration Act 1925, s 58(3) and Land Registration Rules 1989, r 6). If this is the only restriction, then the wife, as surviving proprietor, can appoint an additional trustee. If, however, the further restriction set out in Precedent 47 is entered, then although the wife, as surviving proprietor, can appoint an additional trustee the consent of the husband's personal representatives will be required.

The appointment of a new trustee takes the form of a transfer from the surviving proprietor to herself and the new trustee. The restriction previously entered on the register will remain unless application is lodged for its withdrawal. A declaration of trust or memorandum off the register should be made by the registered proprietors so that it is clear how the net proceeds of sale are to be dealt with following the termination of the trust (usually the death or remarriage of the wife).

(c) Steps to be taken following completion

   (i) *Stamp duty*—No 'PD Form' will be required in connection with either a conveyance/transfer to the wife outright or in connection with the appointment of new trustees as there has been no conveyance on sale. Stamp duty is no longer required on any deed of appointment (Finance Act 1985, s 85). The conveyance to the wife or to trustees will not require a certificate of value but 50p stamp duty will be payable (see Chapter 2 p 24).

   (ii) *Memorandum*—A memorandum of any court order will be endorsed on the original grant of representation to the husband's estate by the court. A memorandum of a conveyance or transfer to trustees, or to the wife, should also be endorsed on the grant and, so far as unregistered land is concerned, a marked copy of such memorandum placed with the title deeds (Administration of Estates Act 1925, s 36).

   (iii) *Court order and completion of abstract*—A marked copy of the court order examined as against the original should be placed with the title documents relating to unregistered land. So far as registered land is concerned, a copy will need to be lodged at the registry when lodging the other documentation.

   (iv) *HM Land Registry fees*—Section 145(2) of The Land Registration Act 1925 provides that where the personal representatives of a deceased person are registered as proprietors on his death (ie when HM Land Registry fees, according to the capital value of the land affected under art 2(5) Land Registration Fees Order 1992 (SI No 2089) are payable claiming abatement 2(e)) a fee is not subsequently chargeable for registering any disposition of the land by them unless the disposition is for valuable consideration. If the personal representatives are not registered as proprietors the transfer from them to the wife is a dealing not for value, so that fees are payable in accordance with Art 2(5) based on the value of the land which was the subject of the dealing less any charge secured thereon (eg by way of mortgage). It is thought that, as this is a transfer of a matrimonial home made pursuant to an order of the court, Abatement 2(i) in Sched 4, Pt I is available, thus reducing the fee to one-fifth with a minimum of £40. So far as an appointment of an additional trustee of the title is concerned, Art 2(5) is again applicable but with Abatement 2(a) applying reducing the fee to one-fifth (with a minimum of £40).

A letter from the solicitor lodging the application certifying the value of the land, will be required, although such certificate seems to be acceptable by completing Form A4 accordingly.

*   *   *   *

PRECEDENTS

A—Conveyance of house in deceased husband's name to wife (or former wife, not remarried) following court order under Inheritance (Provision for Family and Dependants) Act 1975. No mortgage

Precedent 84—Unregistered Land

THIS CONVEYANCE is made the   day of   19
BETWEEN (1) [X] of   and [Y] of   ('the
Executors') and (2) [Wife] of   ('the Wife')

WHEREAS:

(A) At the date of his death [Husband] ('the Testator') was entitled to the Property herein described and conveyed for an estate in fee simple in possession [subject as hereinafter mentioned but otherwise] free from incumbrances

(B) The Testator died on   19   and probate of his will
dated   was on the   day of   granted
to the Executors out of the [District] Probate Registry

(C) By an Order of [Deputy] District Judge   in the
                County Court dated   in proceedings
between the Wife and the Executors bearing number   the
Executors were ordered to convey the Property to the Wife for an estate
in fee simple

(D) The Executors have not given or made any previous assent or
conveyance in respect of the Property or any part thereof

NOW pursuant to the Order THIS DEED WITNESSES:

1 THE Executors as personal representatives of the Testator convey to
the Wife ALL THAT *etc* TO HOLD the same to the Wife in fee simple
[SUBJECT (*continue as Precedent 1, clause 1 if applicable*)]

2 THE Executors ACKNOWLEDGE the right of the Wife to production of the probate of the will of the Testator and to delivery of copies
thereof

[3 *Covenant for indemnity if applicable*
   The Wife covenants with the Executors and each of them that she will
observe and perform the said covenants and conditions and will keep the
Executors and each of them and their respective estates and effects and
the estate and effects of the Testator effectually indemnified against all
losses resulting from their non-observance or breach so far as aforesaid.

IN WITNESS *etc*

Precedent 85 — Registered Land

[Same heading as Precedent 2]

Date   Pursuant to an Order of [Deputy] District Judge
          in the   County Court dated   in
proceedings between the Transferee and the Transferors bearing
number
We [X] of   and [Y] of   ('the Transferors') as
personal representatives of [*Husband*] late of   transfer to
[*Wife*] of   ('the Transferee') the land comprised in the title
above mentioned

[*Covenant for indemnity if applicable*
   The Transferee covenants with the Transferors and each of them that
she will observe and perform the covenants and conditions referred to in
the Charges Register so far as still subsisting and relate to the property
and will keep the Transferors and each of them and their respective
estates and effects and the estate and effects of [*Husband*] effectually
indemnified against all losses resulting from their non-observance or
breach so far as aforesaid]

SIGNED *etc*

B — Appointment of new trustee of conveyance, husband as one of two tenants in common having died

Precedent 86 — Unregistered Land

THIS DEED OF APPOINTMENT is made the   day of
19   BETWEEN (1) [*Wife*] of   ('the Appointor') and
(2) [*AB*] of   ('the New Trustee')

WHEREAS:

(A) By a Conveyance ('the Conveyance') dated   and made between (1) [*XYZ*] and (2) [*Husband*] and the Appointor the property described in the Schedule was conveyed to the said [*Husband*] and the Appointor in fee simple upon trust to sell the same and to hold the net income until sale and the net proceeds of sale in trust for themselves as tenants in common in [equal] shares

[OR, *if the property was conveyed to husband and wife as beneficial joint tenants and the tenancy was subsequently severed*

(A) By a Conveyance ('the Conveyance') dated   and made between (1) [*XYZ*] and (2) [*Husband*] and the Appointor the property described in the Schedule was conveyed to the said [*Husband*] and the Appointor in fee simple upon trust to sell the same and to hold the net income until sale and the net proceeds of sale upon trust for themselves as beneficial joint tenants]

(B) By a notice in writing dated   and given by the said [*Husband*] to the Appointor the said [*Husband*] terminated the beneficial joint tenancy created between the said [*Husband*] and the Appointor by the Conveyance

(B) or (C) [*Husband*] died on

(C) or (D) The Appointor is desirous of appointing the New Trustee to be a trustee of the trusts of the Conveyance jointly with the Appointor and in place of [*Husband*]

NOW THIS DEED WITNESSES that the Appointor in exercise of the statutory power and every other power so enabling her APPOINTS the New Trustee to be a trustee of the trusts of the Conveyance jointly with the Appointor and in place of [*Husband*]

IN WITNESS *etc*

THE SCHEDULE before referred to
[*description of property from
conveyance to the former husband and wife*]

Precedent 87—Registered Land

[Same heading as Precedent 2]

Date 1 For the purpose of effecting an appointment of a New Trustee I, *[Wife]* of transfer to myself the said *[Wife]* and of the land comprised in the title above mentioned *[Husband]* having died on

2 [[*XY*] and [*Z*] as personal representatives of the said *[Husband]* hereby signify their consent to this transfer]

3 It is certified that this instrument falls within category A in the Schedule to The Stamp Duty (Exempt Instruments) Regulations 1987

SIGNED *etc*

Index

179